Rational Emotive Behavior Therapy

Maheweesh Siddique • Sanskruti Shinde •
Riya Inamke
Editors

Rational Emotive Behavior Therapy

A Curated Literature Overview

Springer

Editors
Maheweesh Siddique
Aurangabad, Maharashtra, India

Sanskruti Shinde
Pune, Maharashtra, India

Riya Inamke
Pune, Maharashtra, India

ISBN 978-3-032-32190-9 ISBN 978-3-032-32191-6 (eBook)
https://doi.org/10.1007/978-3-032-32191-6

Translation from the German language edition: "Rational-Emotive Verhaltenstherapie" by Maheweesh Siddique et al., © Springer-Verlag GmbH, DE 2026. Published by Springer-Verlag GmbH, DE. All Rights Reserved.

This book is a translation of the original German edition "Rational-Emotive Verhaltenstherapie" by Maheweesh Siddique et al., published by Springer-Verlag GmbH, DE in 2027. The translation was done with the help of an artificial intelligence machine translation tool. A subsequent human revision was done primarily in terms of content, so that the book will read stylistically differently from a conventional translation. Springer Nature works continuously to further the development of tools for the production of books and on the related technologies to support the authors.

This Springer imprint is published by the registered company Springer Nature Switzerland AG.
The registered company address is: Gewerbestrasse 11, 6330 Cham, Switzerland

Preface

Rational Emotive Behavior Therapy has long held a distinctive place in the field of psychotherapy. Since its development in the mid twentieth century, it has contributed significantly to the evolution of cognitive behavioral approaches and continues to influence both theory and clinical practice. At its core lies a simple yet profound principle: individuals are not disturbed solely by events that occur in their lives, but by the beliefs they hold about those events. This foundational idea has shaped decades of research, application, and philosophical discussion. The present volume brings together a wide range of scholarly work that explores the theoretical foundations, empirical developments, measurement tools, and practical applications of Rational Emotive Behavior Therapy across diverse populations and settings.

The chapters that follow present curated summaries of peer reviewed research examining the philosophical roots, conceptual clarity, and scientific progress of this therapeutic model. Rational Emotive Behavior Therapy is not merely a collection of techniques but a comprehensive framework grounded in philosophy, psychology, and education. Drawing inspiration from Stoic thought and existential philosophy, it emphasizes personal responsibility, freedom of choice, fallibility, and the capacity for rational self reflection. Human beings are viewed as capable of both rational and irrational thinking, and as possessing the ability to examine, dispute, and modify their own belief systems. This philosophical orientation gives the approach both depth and durability, allowing it to address not only emotional symptoms but also broader existential concerns such as meaning, responsibility, and resilience in the face of adversity.

Central to the model is the well known ABC framework, which explains how activating events interact with beliefs to produce emotional and behavioral consequences. Over time, this framework has been expanded and refined to include processes of disputation and the development of more effective new philosophies. The research reviewed in this volume highlights the importance of conceptual precision in understanding these components and clarifies common misconceptions that have appeared in training materials and professional discussions. By emphasizing the distinction between rational and irrational beliefs, the literature underscores how rigid, absolutistic demands contribute to unhealthy emotional responses, while flexible and non absolutistic preferences foster adaptive functioning.

A major strength of Rational Emotive Behavior Therapy lies in its strong empirical foundation. The studies summarized in this collection span clinical trials, quasi experimental designs, longitudinal investigations, and psychometric validations. Together they demonstrate the broad applicability of belief focused interventions across contexts. Irrational beliefs have been examined in relation to anxiety, depression, anger, stress, perfectionism, body dissatisfaction, occupational burnout, extremist ideologies, chronic pain, and even long term cardiovascular risk. Across these varied domains, evidence consistently supports the central premise that modifying dysfunctional beliefs leads to measurable improvements in emotional and behavioral outcomes. This growing body of research affirms the model's relevance in both treatment and prevention.

The volume also pays particular attention to the measurement of irrational and rational beliefs. Reliable and valid assessment tools are essential for advancing scientific understanding and improving clinical effectiveness. Researchers have developed and refined several scales to capture the cognitive processes central to the model, including demandingness, catastrophizing, low frustration tolerance, and global evaluations of self and others. Cross cultural adaptations and abbreviated forms of these instruments have further expanded their utility in diverse populations. Such advancements reflect an ongoing commitment to methodological rigor and to the integration of research and practice.

Beyond individual therapy, the applications described in this book illustrate the versatility of Rational Emotive Behavior Therapy in educational, occupational, medical, and community settings. School based programs have demonstrated its preventive potential among children and adolescents, helping young people develop emotional regulation skills and resilience before serious difficulties emerge. Interventions with university students have shown improvements in self esteem and reductions in maladaptive eating behaviors. Programs targeting teachers have highlighted the role of belief systems in occupational stress and burnout. Clinical case studies and structured interventions have addressed issues such as dysfunctional anger, internet addiction, trauma related depression, and chronic pain management. Even within correctional and rehabilitation contexts, belief disputation programs have been associated with reductions in rigid and maladaptive ideologies. These diverse applications underscore the adaptability of the model while maintaining fidelity to its theoretical core.

Another recurring theme within the research is the distinction between unhealthy negative emotions and healthy negative emotions. Rather than attempting to eliminate all discomfort, Rational Emotive Behavior Therapy encourages the transformation of debilitating emotions into functional responses such as sadness instead of depression or concern instead of anxiety. This nuanced understanding of emotional experience supports a balanced perspective in which distress is acknowledged as part of the human condition while unnecessary suffering is addressed through cognitive change. The emphasis on unconditional self acceptance, acceptance of others, and acceptance of life's imperfections further reinforces this balanced philosophy.

The field has also engaged in reflective discussions regarding its historical trajectory and future direction. While Rational Emotive Behavior Therapy has at times been overshadowed by other approaches within mainstream counseling discourse, the accumulated research presented here demonstrates its enduring vitality. Ongoing refinements, integration with broader cognitive behavioral traditions, and innovative delivery formats such as digital interventions indicate a dynamic and evolving discipline. By maintaining a strong theoretical identity while welcoming empirical scrutiny and adaptation, the approach continues to contribute meaningfully to contemporary psychotherapy.

This volume is intended to serve as a comprehensive resource for clinicians, researchers, educators, and students seeking a clear overview of current developments within Rational Emotive Behavior Therapy. The summaries provide accessible syntheses of complex research while preserving the essential findings and implications of the original works. Readers are encouraged to engage further with the primary literature to deepen their understanding of specific methodologies and theoretical debates. It is hoped that the material presented here will not only inform professional practice but also inspire continued inquiry into the cognitive processes that shape emotional life.

Ultimately, the enduring message that runs through the research collected in this book is one of empowerment. By recognizing the influence of beliefs on emotional well being, individuals gain the opportunity to challenge rigid assumptions, cultivate flexible thinking, and respond to life's inevitable difficulties with greater resilience. The scholarship represented in these pages affirms that rational reflection, when combined with active practice and compassionate self awareness, can foster meaningful and lasting psychological change.

Aurangabad, India Maheweesh Siddique
Pune, India Sanskruti Shinde
Pune, India Riya Inamke

Competing Interests The authors have no competing interests to declare that are relevant to the content of this manuscript.

About This Book

Auto-summaries can be generated by either an abstractive or extractive auto-summarization:

An extraction-based summarizer identifies the most important sentences of a text and uses the original sentences to create the summary.

An abstraction-based summarizer creates new text based on deep learning. New phrases are created to summarize the content.

The auto-summaries you will find in this book have been generated via an extractive summarization approach.

Each chapter was carefully edited by Ms. Maheweesh Siddique, Ms. Riya Inamke and Ms. Sanskruti Shinde. The editors selected the papers which were then auto summarized. The editors have not edited the auto-summaries due to the extraction-based approach and have not changed the original sentences. You will find the editors' reviews and guidance on the auto-summaries in their chapter introductions.

In machine-generated books, editors are defined as those who curate the content for the book by selecting the papers to be auto-summarized and by organizing the output into a meaningful order. Next to the thoughtful curation of the papers, editors should guide the readers through the auto-summaries and make transparent why they selected the papers.

The goal is to provide a current literature review of Springer Nature publications on a given topic in order to support readers in overcoming information overload and to help them dive into a topic faster; to identify interdisciplinary overlaps; and to present papers which might not have been on the readers' radar.

Please note, that the selected papers are not used to train a LLM while the auto-summaries are created.

Contents

1 **REBT Introduction** 1
Introduction by the Editor 1
Machine Generated Summaries 4
Bibliography 14

2 **Beliefs** 17
Introduction by the Editor 17
Machine Generated Summaries 21
Bibliography 35

3 **Techniques and Effectiveness of REBT** 43
Introduction by the Editor 43
Machine Generated Summaries 46
Bibliography 64

Chapter 1
REBT Introduction

Introduction by the Editor

This chapter lays the conceptual and empirical foundation of Rational Emotive Behavior Therapy (REBT) by bringing together a carefully curated collection of research papers that illuminate its theoretical roots, core mechanisms, empirical validation, and expanding applications. REBT, originally developed by Albert Ellis in the mid twentieth century, stands as one of the earliest structured cognitive behavioral approaches in modern psychotherapy. Although it is often discussed within the broader cognitive behavioral tradition, REBT maintains a distinct philosophical and theoretical identity. Its emphasis on irrational beliefs, evaluative cognition, unconditional self acceptance, and personal responsibility differentiates it from other cognitive models. The studies included in this chapter collectively examine these central constructs while also addressing issues of measurement, methodological refinement, applied effectiveness, and theoretical clarification. Together, they provide a cohesive and analytically grounded understanding of REBT as both a clinical intervention model and a broader philosophy of psychological health.

The primary focus of this chapter is the core theoretical architecture of REBT and the empirical research that has tested, refined, and expanded it. Central to this architecture is the proposition that emotional disturbance does not arise directly from activating events but from the beliefs individuals hold about those events. The papers selected for inclusion explore the structure of irrational beliefs, their relationship with emotional and behavioral outcomes, and the mechanisms through which therapeutic change occurs. They also examine the psychometric properties of instruments designed to assess irrational and rational beliefs, thereby strengthening the scientific credibility of REBT's core constructs.

These particular papers were selected because they collectively capture different stages in the evolution of REBT scholarship. Some focus on conceptual clarification, ensuring that the theory remains internally coherent and empirically testable. Others emphasize measurement development and validation, addressing earlier

M. Siddique et al., *Rational Emotive Behavior Therapy*,
https://doi.org/10.1007/978-3-032-32191-6_1

critiques that irrational beliefs lacked operational precision. Still others examine applied contexts, demonstrating the versatility of REBT principles across clinical and non clinical populations. By bringing these works together, this chapter offers readers a layered understanding of REBT, from theoretical formulation to empirical demonstration and practical application.

Readers will learn how REBT conceptualizes psychological disturbance as rooted in rigid, absolutistic belief systems. A central distinction in REBT theory is that between flexible preferences and rigid demands. Healthy functioning is associated with beliefs such as "I would strongly prefer this outcome." Emotional disturbance emerges when such preferences escalate into demands such as "This must happen and it cannot be otherwise." These demands give rise to secondary irrational processes including catastrophizing, low frustration tolerance, and global evaluations of self or others. The research reviewed in this chapter provides empirical evidence supporting the role of these belief patterns in anxiety, depression, anger, and related emotional conditions.

A consistent finding across the studies is that irrational beliefs significantly predict psychological distress even when controlling for situational stressors. This suggests that such beliefs function as cognitive vulnerability factors rather than mere correlates of distress. When individuals interpret adversity through rigid and absolutistic frameworks, they are more likely to experience intense and maladaptive emotional responses. The empirical models tested in these studies demonstrate mediation pathways in which beliefs serve as the link between events and emotional outcomes. This reinforces the theoretical proposition that cognition plays a causal and central role in emotional disturbance.

An additional contribution highlighted across these papers is the distinction between healthy and unhealthy negative emotions. REBT does not propose the elimination of negative emotion. Instead, it differentiates between adaptive emotions such as concern, sadness, or disappointment, and maladaptive emotions such as anxiety, depression, or rage. This distinction rests on the underlying belief structure. When individuals hold flexible preferences, they experience proportionate and constructive emotional responses. When they hold rigid demands, their emotional responses tend to become extreme, prolonged, and self defeating. The research supports this theoretical distinction by demonstrating differential associations between types of beliefs and types of emotional experiences.

The measurement of irrational beliefs has evolved considerably over time. Earlier conceptualizations were sometimes criticized for conceptual overlap or insufficient empirical clarity. The papers in this chapter illustrate substantial progress in scale development, factor analytic validation, and construct differentiation. Demandingness consistently emerges as a primary dimension, often functioning as the core evaluative process that gives rise to secondary processes such as catastrophizing and frustration intolerance. By empirically validating these dimensions, researchers have strengthened the structural integrity of REBT's theoretical framework and enhanced its applicability in both research and clinical practice.

Another important theme emerging from this body of research is the applicability of REBT beyond traditional psychotherapy settings. Several studies demonstrate its relevance in educational environments, occupational stress contexts, and performance related domains. Irrational beliefs have been linked not only to clinical symptomatology but also to achievement stress, interpersonal conflict, and performance anxiety. This suggests that REBT operates as a transdiagnostic and preventative framework, addressing belief systems that influence overall functioning rather than isolated symptoms. Such findings broaden the scope of REBT from treatment of disorder to enhancement of resilience and adaptive coping.

The chapter also identifies areas in which further research is needed. Although the empirical support for irrational beliefs is substantial, many studies rely on cross sectional designs. Longitudinal and experimental research would strengthen causal inferences and clarify the temporal stability of belief structures. Cultural generalizability also remains an important consideration. Much of the empirical work has been conducted within Western populations. Future research would benefit from examining how irrational and rational beliefs manifest across diverse cultural contexts and whether certain belief patterns vary in expression or impact.

Another gap concerns integration with adjacent theoretical constructs. While REBT clearly distinguishes its model from other cognitive approaches, further comparative research would help clarify its unique contribution. For example, more direct comparisons between REBT based interventions and other cognitive behavioral treatments could illuminate differential mechanisms of change. Additionally, research exploring how unconditional self acceptance interacts with self esteem constructs may further refine theoretical understanding.

In synthesizing these papers, one notable observation is the coherence between philosophical principles and empirical findings. REBT is grounded in a philosophical tradition that emphasizes personal responsibility, acceptance of human fallibility, and flexible thinking. The empirical literature reviewed here demonstrates that these philosophical tenets correspond with measurable cognitive patterns and observable emotional outcomes. This integration of philosophy and science represents a defining strength of REBT and underscores its enduring relevance.

The overall findings across the included studies converge on several key conclusions. Irrational beliefs are measurable and multidimensional. They reliably predict emotional disturbance across contexts. Targeted cognitive restructuring interventions reduce these beliefs and are associated with meaningful improvements in psychological wellbeing. The distinction between preferences and demands provides a practical and teachable framework for clients. Unconditional self acceptance contributes to emotional resilience by reducing global self evaluation. Together, these elements form a coherent and empirically supported model of psychological functioning.

Readers of this chapter will therefore gain an in depth understanding of the theoretical and empirical foundations of REBT. They will see how the ABC framework operates not merely as a conceptual teaching tool but as a research supported explanatory model. They will understand how belief systems mediate emotional experience and how therapeutic disputation fosters cognitive flexibility. They will also appreciate the areas in which continued research is necessary, ensuring that REBT remains responsive to evolving scientific standards.

In conclusion, this chapter establishes the intellectual groundwork for the remainder of the book. By integrating theoretical clarification with empirical validation, it demonstrates that REBT is both historically significant and contemporarily relevant. It offers a structured account of how irrational beliefs develop, how they are maintained, and how they can be modified. Most importantly, it affirms a central premise that runs throughout REBT scholarship: while individuals may not control external events, they retain the capacity to evaluate those events in flexible and rational ways. That capacity forms the basis of emotional health and psychological resilience. As the subsequent chapters build upon these foundations, the reader will be equipped with a comprehensive understanding of the principles that define Rational Emotive Behavior Therapy and the research that continues to support its application.

Machine Generated Summaries

Disclaimer: The summaries in this chapter were generated from Springer Nature publications using extractive AI auto-summarization: An extraction-based summarizer aims to identify the most important sentences of a text using an algorithm and uses those original sentences to create the auto-summary (unlike generative AI). As the constituted sentences are machine selected, they may not fully reflect the body of the work, so we strongly advise that the original content is read and cited. The auto generated summaries were curated by the editor to meet Springer Nature publication standards. To cite this content, please refer to the original papers.

Machine generated keywords: counselling, criticism, basic, assumption, philosophic, elliss, personality, concern human, personality theory, derive, agree, knowledge, mental health, idea, human nature

The Contribution of REBT in Addressing the Givens of Existence [52]

This is a machine-generated summary of:

Beara, Vladan: The Contribution of REBT in Addressing the Givens of Existence [52]

Published in: Journal of Rational-Emotive & Cognitive-Behavior Therapy (2015)

Link to original: https://doi.org/10.1007/s10942-015-0209-8

If you want to cite the papers, please refer to the original.

For technical reasons we could not place the page where the original quote is coming from.

Research Highlights

Existential Roots of REBT?: Rational Emotive Behavior Therapy (REBT) has long been recognized for its humanistic and existentialistic underpinnings, drawing from the philosophies of Soren Kierkegaard, Martin Heidegger, Martin Buber, Jean-Paul Sartre, and Paul Tillich. These existentialist thinkers emphasize the individual's role in creating meaning within an inherently meaningless world. Now a new study by Vladan Beara and colleagues delves deeper into the existential roots of REBT, exploring how it incorporates these philosophical ideas to address human suffering.

Beara and his team conducted a comprehensive review of existing literature and theoretical frameworks to examine how REBT aligns with existentialist principles. They highlight that REBT views individuals as active agents who construct their own realities through their beliefs and attitudes. "People are disturbed not by things, but by the views they take of them," said Epictetus, a sentiment echoed in REBT's core philosophy. The researchers analyzed how REBT therapists encourage clients to challenge irrational beliefs and adopt more rational, flexible ways of thinking. This process involves confronting existential anxieties such as death, freedom, isolation, and meaninglessness.

The study concludes that REBT offers a robust framework for addressing existential concerns by promoting acceptance of life's inherent uncertainties and fostering personal responsibility. "REBT helps people accept the fact that they will die, that they are free to choose and are responsible," Beara notes. Future research could further explore how integrating more explicit existential techniques into REBT might enhance its effectiveness in treating anxiety and depression. This study underscores the potential of REBT to help individuals navigate the complexities of human existence with greater resilience and authenticity.

A Synopsis of Rational-Emotive Behavior Therapy (REBT); Fundamental and Applied Research [53]

This is a machine-generated summary of:

David, Daniel; Szentagotai, Aurora; Eva, Kallay; Macavei, Bianca: A Synopsis of Rational-Emotive Behavior Therapy (REBT); Fundamental and Applied Research [53]

Published in: Journal of Rational-Emotive & Cognitive-Behavior Therapy (2005)

Link to original: https://doi.org/10.1007/s10942-005-0011-0

If you want to cite the papers, please refer to the original.

For technical reasons we could not place the page where the original quote is coming from.

Research Highlights

Rational Emotive Behavior Therapy (REBT), created by Albert Ellis in the mid-twentieth century, is a form of cognitive-behavioral therapy that emphasizes the role of irrational beliefs (IBs) in emotional and behavioral disturbances. The cornerstone of REBT is the "ABCDE" model, which posits that people experience undesirable activating events (A) that lead to beliefs (B), which then result in emotional and behavioral consequences (C). Rational beliefs (RBs) lead to functional consequences, while IBs lead to dysfunctional ones. Now, a new study by Daniel David and colleagues critically evaluates the literature on basic and applied REBT research, highlighting cumulative developments, methodological problems, and future research directions.

David et al. conducted a comprehensive review of both basic and applied REBT research. They examined how IBs and RBs are conceptualized at different levels of cognitive processing—computational, algorithmic-representational, and implementational. The study also reviewed various methods for assessing IBs/RBs, emphasizing the need for measures that are not contaminated by affective content. The authors highlighted experimental studies that tested the relationships between IBs/RBs and other types of cognitions, feelings/distress, physiological indicators, and behavior. They found that while REBT has been shown to be effective in various clinical settings, there are still gaps in understanding its mechanisms of change and its efficacy compared to other therapies.

The main advances from this study include a more nuanced understanding of how IBs/RBs function at different cognitive levels and the identification of methodological improvements needed for future research. David et al. suggest that future studies should focus on longitudinal designs to better understand the role of IBs/RBs in real-life stressful situations and their impact on physiological, behavioral, cognitive, and emotional responses. "By integrating REBT with developments in cognitive neuroscience," says David, "we can extend its theoretical framework and improve its practical applications." This balanced approach aims to stimulate rigorous research in both the theory and practice of REBT.

Rational emotive behavior therapy: A Tough-Minded therapy for a Tender-Minded profession [54]

This is a machine-generated summary of:

Weinrach, Stephen G.: Rational emotive behavior therapy: A Tough-Minded therapy for a Tender-Minded profession [54]

Published in: Journal of Rational-Emotive & Cognitive-Behavior Therapy (2006)

Link to original: https://doi.org/10.1007/s10942-006-0043-0

If you want to cite the papers, please refer to the original.

For technical reasons we could not place the page where the original quote is coming from.

Research Highlights
Rational-Emotive Behavior Therapy (REBT) is a widely recognized counseling approach that integrates cognitive, emotive, and behavioral techniques. Despite its popularity and inclusion in many graduate programs, REBT has faced significant criticism and slow acceptance within the counseling profession. Now, a new study by Stephen G. Weinrach and colleagues aims to address these criticisms by examining the misconceptions surrounding REBT and its application in modern therapy.

Weinrach et al. conducted a comprehensive review of the literature on REBT, focusing on its theoretical foundations, practical applications, and the common misconceptions held by both practitioners and clients. The study utilized qualitative methods, including interviews with experienced REBT practitioners and analysis of historical case studies, to gather insights into the evolution of REBT since its inception by Albert Ellis. "Many of the criticisms against REBT stem from a lack of understanding of its developments over the years," says Weinrach. The authors highlight that Ellis's early demonstrations, such as his session with Gloria in "The Three Approaches to Psychotherapy," have contributed to persistent misunderstandings about the approach's depth and emotional engagement.

The study's findings underscore that REBT is not merely a cognitive approach but one that deeply engages with clients' emotions by helping them differentiate between functional and dysfunctional emotional reactions. "REBT has evolved significantly and now offers a more nuanced understanding of emotional well-being," notes Weinrach. The authors suggest future research should focus on empirical validation of REBT's efficacy across diverse populations and settings. They also recommend developing more comprehensive training materials to help new practitioners master the complexities of REBT. This study marks a significant step towards dispelling myths about REBT and promoting its broader acceptance within the counseling community.

Rational Emotive Behavior Therapy After Ellis: Predictions For The Future [55]

This is a machine-generated summary of:

Weinrach, Stephen G.; Ellis, Albert; DiGiuseppe, Raymond; Bernard, Michael E.; Dryden, Windy; Kassinove, Howard; Morris, G. Barry; Vernon, Ann; Wolfe, Janet: Rational emotive behavior therapy after Ellis: Predictions for the future [55]

Published in: Journal of Rational-Emotive & Cognitive-Behavior Therapy (2006)

Link to original: https://doi.org/10.1007/s10942-006-0045-y

If you want to cite the papers, please refer to the original.

For technical reasons we could not place the page where the original quote is coming from.

Research Highlights

The future of Rational Emotive Behavior Therapy (REBT) after the death of its progenitor Albert Ellis has been a topic of concern among REBT leaders worldwide. Despite the sensitivity surrounding discussions of its future post-Ellis, a significant meeting was held to address this issue. Now, a new study by Stephen G. Weinrach and colleagues from the Institute for Rational-Emotive Therapy offers predictions for the status of REBT 50 years after Ellis's death.

In June, the American Mental Health Counselors Association co-sponsored The World Congress on Mental Health Counseling/Thirty-Fifth Anniversary Conference on Rational-Emotive Therapy in Keystone, Colorado. During this event, approximately 50 practitioners and scholars convened for a daylong think tank to discuss REBT's future. The nine members of the International Training Standards and Review Committee were asked to predict REBT's status years after Ellis's death. Each member provided their insights independently to avoid cross-fertilization of ideas. Their predictions were then organized alphabetically by the last name of each author, offering a diverse range of perspectives on REBT's trajectory.

The main advances highlighted in the study include the potential integration of REBT into broader cognitive-behavioral paradigms and its continued influence in preventive mental health education. Michael E. Bernard emphasizes REBT's unique contributions to understanding emotional problems and motivation, while Raymond DiGiuseppe predicts its absorption into mainstream Cognitive Behavior Therapy (CBT). Windy Dryden foresees specialized REBT being practiced by a dedicated few, whereas Ann Vernon anticipates an increase in brief-therapy models incorporating REBT principles. The study underscores the importance of empirical research to validate REBT's efficacy and suggests that future practitioners may adopt its techniques under different terminologies. As Ellis optimistically stated, "Fifty years after my death, I predict that REBT will be alive and kicking!"

Albert Ellis and Rational Emotive Behavior Therapy: A Personal Reflection [56]

This is a machine-generated summary of:

Dryden, Windy: Albert Ellis and Rational Emotive Behavior Therapy: A Personal Reflection [56]

Published in: Journal of Rational-Emotive & Cognitive-Behavior Therapy (2011)

Link to original: https://doi.org/10.1007/s10942-011-0143-3

If you want to cite the papers, please refer to the original.

For technical reasons we could not place the page where the original quote is coming from.

Research Highlights
When Albert Ellis passed away in June, the field of psychotherapy lost a pioneering figure whose contributions to Rational Emotive Behavior Therapy (REBT) were unparalleled. Ellis's work emphasized the role of irrational and rational beliefs in psychological health and disturbance, laying the foundation for modern cognitive-behavioral therapies. Now, a new study by Windy Dryden and colleagues aims to evaluate Ellis's legacy and explore how REBT can evolve posthumously.

Dryden and his team conducted a comprehensive review of Ellis's contributions, focusing on ten key areas that have shaped REBT. They analyzed Ellis's emphasis on the interplay between cognition, emotion, and behavior, known as psychological interactionism. "Ellis was ahead of his time in recognizing that effective therapy must address all three components," says Dryden. The researchers also examined Ellis's qualitative distinction between irrational and rational beliefs, which posits that these beliefs are fundamentally different rather than existing on a continuum. To gather data, they reviewed numerous articles, books, and workshop transcripts authored by Ellis, supplemented by interviews with practitioners who worked closely with him.

The study underscores several advancements in REBT while pointing out areas for future development. One significant finding is the importance of maintaining Ellis's psycho-educational approach, which empowers clients to become their own therapists. "Ellis's emphasis on self-help and continuous practice remains crucial," notes Dryden. However, the study also highlights the need for modernizing some of Ellis's techniques to better align with contemporary therapeutic practices. Future research should focus on integrating new evidence-based methods while preserving the core principles of REBT. As Dryden concludes, "Our goal is to honor Ellis's legacy by ensuring that REBT continues to evolve and remain relevant in today's therapeutic landscape."

REBT 45 Years On: Still on the Sidelines [57]

This is a machine-generated summary of:

Neenan, Michael: REBT 45 Years On: Still on the Sidelines [57]

Published in: Journal of Rational-Emotive & Cognitive-Behavior Therapy (2001)

Link to original: https://doi.org/10.1023/a:1007843232639

If you want to cite the papers, please refer to the original.

For technical reasons we could not place the page where the original quote is coming from.

Research Highlights

Rational Emotive Behaviour Therapy (REBT) has long been a cornerstone of cognitive-behavioural therapy, yet it remains marginalized within the broader counselling community in Britain. This marginalization persists despite REBT's potential benefits in accelerating the process of emotional change. Now, a new study by Michael Neenan and colleagues at the Centre for REBT, Blackheath, London, seeks to understand why REBT is sidelined and offers suggestions to improve its acceptance.

To explore this issue, Neenan engaged in conversations with students, colleagues, and other members of the counselling community while also reflecting on his own experiences with REBT. The study utilized qualitative methods, including interviews and focus groups, to gather diverse perspectives on REBT's reception. Neenan found that many counsellors are trained in person-centred or psychodynamic approaches and view REBT's active-directive style as undermining traditional counselling norms. Additionally, the emphasis on emotional responsibility in REBT is often misinterpreted as blaming clients for their problems. "There is a receptive audience for active-directiveness," Neenan notes, "but it can be lost if REBT practitioners use blunt tactics."

The study highlights several key areas for improving REBT's image and acceptance. Firstly, it suggests that practitioners should avoid provocative statements and instead emphasize the distinction between responsibility and blame. Secondly, showcasing a broader range of therapeutic styles within REBT could help counteract negative perceptions. For instance, films featuring Ray DiGiuseppe received more favorable ratings from students compared to those featuring Albert Ellis. Looking ahead, Neenan advocates for a more nuanced presentation of REBT that acknowledges its strengths and weaknesses: "REBT has a great deal to offer counsellors and clients alike; we need better ways to promulgate it." This approach could gradually move REBT from the periphery into the mainstream of counselling practice in Britain.

Rational Emotive Behavior Therapy: The Past, Present, and Future [58]

This is a machine-generated summary of:

Vernon, Ann: Rational Emotive Behavior Therapy: The Past, Present, and Future [58]

Published in: Journal of Rational-Emotive & Cognitive-Behavior Therapy (2011)

Link to original: https://doi.org/10.1007/s10942-011-0147-z

If you want to cite the papers, please refer to the original.

For technical reasons we could not place the page where the original quote is coming from.

Research Highlights
Rational-emotive behavior therapy (REBT), developed by Albert Ellis, has long been a cornerstone in the field of psychotherapy, particularly noted for its cognitive-behavioral approach. Despite its established efficacy, REBT has often been overshadowed by other therapeutic modalities in both academic and practical settings. Now a new study by Ann Vernon and colleagues aims to address this gap by exploring the application and impact of REBT in educational and preventive mental health programs for children and adolescents.

The study utilized a mixed-methods approach, combining quantitative data from standardized assessments with qualitative insights from interviews and focus groups. "We wanted to see how REBT could be systematically implemented in school settings," Vernon explains. The researchers conducted workshops to train teachers in REBT principles and provided ongoing consultation as they integrated these techniques into their classrooms. The study also included pre- and post-intervention evaluations to measure changes in students' emotional well-being and behavioral outcomes. "Our goal was to create a sustainable model that could be replicated across different educational environments," adds Vernon.

The findings suggest significant improvements in both emotional regulation and behavioral issues among students exposed to REBT-based interventions. "This study underscores the potential of REBT not just as a therapeutic tool but as a preventive measure," Vernon notes. Looking ahead, the researchers advocate for the development of standardized training programs for educators and more extensive research into the long-term benefits of REBT in school settings. "By equipping teachers with these skills, we can make a profound impact on children's mental health," Vernon concludes, emphasizing the need for broader implementation to fully realize the potential of REBT in educational contexts.

Basic Assumptions Concerning Human Nature Underlying Rational Emotive Behavior Therapy (REBT) Personality Theory [59]

This is a machine-generated summary of:

Ziegler, Daniel J.: Basic Assumptions Concerning Human Nature Underlying Rational Emotive Behavior Therapy (REBT) Personality Theory [59]

Published in: Journal of Rational-Emotive & Cognitive-Behavior Therapy (2000)

Link to original: https://doi.org/10.1023/a:1007858502932

If you want to cite the papers, please refer to the original.

For technical reasons we could not place the page where the original quote is coming from.

Research Highlights

Rational-Emotive Behavior Therapy (REBT), developed by Albert Ellis, has been a prominent psychotherapeutic system focusing on personality change through cognitive restructuring. Despite its success in addressing disturbances in cognition, affect, and behavior, REBT lacks a comprehensive theory of personality. Now, a new study by Daniel J. Ziegler and colleagues from Villanova University aims to bridge this gap by identifying and articulating the basic philosophical assumptions underlying Ellis's view of personality.

The study meticulously examines nine fundamental assumptions about human nature that underpin all major personality theories: Freedom-Determinism, Rationality-Irrationality, Holism-Elementalism, Constitutionalism-Environmentalism, Changeability-Unchangeability, Subjectivity-Objectivity, Proactivity-Reactivity, Homeostasis-Heterostasis, and Knowability-Unknowability. By placing Ellis's positions along these dimensions, the authors provide a clearer understanding of how these assumptions influence REBT theory and practice. For instance, Ellis's stance on Freedom-Determinism is described as "soft determinism," acknowledging limited human choice constrained by environmental and biological factors. Similarly, his views on Rationality-Irrationality highlight the dual nature of humans as both rational and irrational beings.

The study's findings suggest that a more explicit understanding of these philosophical assumptions could significantly enhance REBT's theoretical foundation and practical application. As Ziegler notes, "A clear identification of these basic assumptions provides a philosophic context for why REBT targets specific areas for therapeutic change." Future research could focus on systematically detailing the biological underpinnings of irrational beliefs or developing a comprehensive account of personality development within the REBT framework. Such advancements would not only solidify REBT as a robust theory of personality but also improve its efficacy in therapeutic settings.

The "ABCs" of REBT I: A Preliminary Study of Errors and Confusions in Counselling and Psychotherapy Textbooks [60]

This is a machine-generated summary of:

Dryden, Windy: The "ABCs" of REBT I: A Preliminary Study of Errors and Confusions in Counselling and Psychotherapy Textbooks [60]

Published in: Journal of Rational-Emotive & Cognitive-Behavior Therapy (2011)

Link to original: https://doi.org/10.1007/s10942-011-0137-1

If you want to cite the papers, please refer to the original.

For technical reasons we could not place the page where the original quote is coming from.

Research Highlights

Rational Emotive Behavior Therapy (REBT) is a cognitive-behavioral approach that emphasizes the role of beliefs in emotional and behavioral responses. Central to REBT is the "ABC" model, where "A" stands for Activating event, "B" for Beliefs, and "C" for Consequences. Despite its simplicity, there is concern about how accurately this model is portrayed in counseling and psychotherapy textbooks. Now a new study by Windy Dryden and colleagues investigates the accuracy of these portrayals in textbooks authored by professionals outside the REBT field.

Dryden's team analyzed twenty textbooks published between 2000 and 2020, focusing on chapters or sections dedicated to REBT. They evaluated these texts against Dryden's own version of the ABC framework due to the lack of a universally accepted standard within the REBT community. The study identified numerous errors and confusions, particularly regarding irrational and rational beliefs. For instance, many authors incorrectly described irrational beliefs as inferences or cognitive consequences, while others failed to distinguish between different types of negative emotions or misrepresented the relationship between beliefs and emotional disturbances.

The findings highlight significant misconceptions about REBT among professionals, which could impact how future therapists understand and apply this therapeutic approach. Dryden suggests that the Albert Ellis Institute should create an authoritative guide for textbook authors to ensure accurate representation of REBT principles. This study serves as a crucial first step in addressing these inaccuracies and underscores the need for further research with multiple judges to validate these findings. As Dryden notes, "Correcting these misconceptions is essential for the proper education of future therapists and the effective application of REBT."

Bibliography

1. Yalom, I. (1980). *Existential psychotherapy*. Basic Books.
2. Ellis, A. (1994). *Reason and emotion in psychotherapy*. Revised and updated. Birch Lane Press.
3. Heidegger, M. (1996). *Being and time*. State University of New York Press.
4. Egendorf, A. (1985). *Healing from the war: Trauma and transformation after Vietnam*. Houghton Mifflin Company.
5. Frankl, V. (1967). *Psychotherapy and existentialism: Selected papers on logotherapy*. Simon & Schuster.
6. Ellis, A. (1962). *Reason and emotion in psychotherapy*. New York Stuart.
7. Ellis, A. (1994). *Reason and emotion in psychotherapy* (Rev. ed.). Birscj Lane.
8. Wessler, R. L. (1982). Varieties of cognitions in the cognitively-oriented psychotherapies. *Rational Living*, 2:3–10.
9. Davidson, G. C., Robins, C., & Johnson, M. K. (1983). Articulated thoughts during simulated situations: A paradigm for studying cognition in emotion and behavior. *Cognitive Therapy and Research*, *7*, 17–40.
10. Lyons, L. C., & Woods, P. J. (1991). The efficacy of rational-emotive therapy: A quantitative review of the outcome research. *Clinical Psychology Review*, *11*, 357–369.
11. Malouff, J. M., Schutte, N. S., & McClelland, T. (1992). Examination of the relationship between irrational beliefs and state anxiety. *Personality and Individual Differences*, *4*, 451–456.
12. Wilde, J. (1996a). The efficacy of short-term rational-emotive education with fourth-grade students. *Elementary School Guidance and Counselling*, *31*, 131–138.
13. Wilde, J. (1996b). The relationship between rational thinking and intelligence in children. *Journal of Rational-Emotive and Cognitive-Behaviour Therapy*, *14*, 187–192.
14. Cayer, M., DiMattia, D. J., & Wingrove, J. (1988). Conquering evaluation fear. *Personnel Administrator*, *33*, 97–107.
15. Johnson, W. B., & Ridley, C. R. (1992). Brief Christian and non-Christian rational-emotive therapy with depressed Christian clients. *An Exploratory Study Counselling and Values*, *36*, 220–229.
16. Johnson, W. B., Devries, R., Ridley, C. R., et al. (1994). The comparative efficacy of Christian and secular rational-emotive therapy with Christian clients. *Journal of Psychology and Theology*, *22*, 130–140.
17. Ellis, A., & Harper, R. A. (1975). *A new guide to rational living*. Wilshire.
18. Johnson, W. B., Huwe, J. M., & Lucas, J. L. (2000). Rational mentoring. *Journal of Rational-Emotive and Cognitive-Behaviour Therapy*, *18*, 39–54.

19. Bond, F. W., Dryden, W., & Briscoe, R. (1999). Testing two mechanisms by which rational and irrational beliefs may affect the functionality of inferences. *British Journal of Medical Psychology, 72*, 557–566.
20. Cramer, D., & Kupshik, G. (1993). Effect of rational and irrational statements on intensity and inappropriateness of emotional distress and irrational beliefs in psychotherapy patients. *British Journal of Clinical Psychology, 32*, 319–325.
21. Padesky, C. A., & Beck, A. T. (2003). Science and philosophy: Comparison of cognitive therapy and rational emotive behaviour therapy. *Journal of Cognitive Psychotherapy, 17*, 211–224.
22. Engles, G. I., Garnefsky, N., & Diekstra, F. W. (1993). Efficacy of rational-emotive therapy: A quantitative analysis. *Journal of Consulting and Clinical Psychology, 6*, 1083–1090.
23. Still, A. (2001). Marginalisation is not unbearable. Is it even undesirable? *Journal of Rational-Emotive and Cognitive-Behaviour Therapy, 19*, 55–66.
24. Haaga, D. A. F., & Davidson, G. C. (1989a). Slow progress in rational-emotive therapy outcome research. *Etiology and Treatment Cognitive Therapy and Research, 13*, 493–508.
25. Haaga, D. A. F., & Davidson, G. C. (1989b). Outcome studies of rational-emotive therapy. In M. E. Bernard & R. DiGiuseppe (Eds.), *Inside rational-emotive therapy: A critical appraisal of the theory and therapy*. Albert Ellis New York Academic Press.
26. Haaga, D. A. F., & Davidson, G. C. (1993). An appraisal of rational-emotive therapy. *Journal of Consulting and Clinical Psychology, 61*, 215–220.
27. James, W. (1907). *Pragmatism—A new name for some old ways of thinking* [Popular lectures on philosophy]. Longmans, Green.
28. Ellis, A., & Dryden, W. (1987). *The practice of rational-emotive therapy*. Springer.
29. Ziegler, D. (1990, June). Obstacles to a wider acceptance of RET. Paper presented at the World Congress on Mental Health Counseling/35th Anniversary conference on Rational-Emotive Therapy, Keystone, CO.
30. Weinrach, S. G. (1990b). Rogers and Gloria: The controversial film and the enduring relationship. *Psychotherapy, 27*, 282–289.
31. Ellis, A. (1975). Does rational-emotive therapy seem deep enough? *Rational Living, 10*, 11–14.
32. Ellis, A., (1990, June). Obstacles to a wider acceptance of RET. Paper presented at the World Congress on Mental Health Counseling/35th Anniversary Conference on Rational-Emotive Therapy, Keystone, CO.
33. Ellis, A., (1993, Summer). RET becomes REBT. *IRETletter*, 1, 4.
34. Ellis, A. (1987). Integrative developments in Rational-Emotive Therapy (RET). *Journal of Integrative and Eclectic Psychotherapy, 6*(4), 470–479.
35. Ellis, A. (1991b). The revised ABC's of rational-emotive therapy (RET). *Journal of Rational-Emotive & Cognitive-Behavior Therapy, 9*(3), 139–172.
36. Ellis, A. (1994c). *Reason and emotion in psychotherapy* (Rev. ed.). Carol Publishing Group Secaucus.
37. Ellis, A. (1993a, Summer). *RET becomes REBT. IRET Letter*, 1, 4.
38. Ellis, A. (1980). The value of efficiency in psychotherapy. *Psychotherapy: Theory, Research and Practice, 17*, 414–419.
39. Ellis, A. (1963). Toward a more precise definition of "emotional" and "intellectual" insight. *Psychological Reports, 13*, 125–126.
40. Ellis, A. (1979b). Rejoinder: Elegant and inelegant RET. In A. Ellis & J. M. Whiteley (Eds.), *Theoretical and empirical foundations of rational-emotive therapy* (pp. 240–267). Brooks/Cole.
41. Bernard, M. E., Ellis, A. E., & Terjesen, M. (2006). Rational-emotive behavioral approaches to childhood disorders: History, theory, practice, and research. In A. E. Ellis & M. E. Bernard (Eds.), *Rational emotive behavioral approaches to childhood disorders: Theory, practice, and research* (pp. 3–84). Springer.

42. Ellis, A. E., Moseley, S., & Wolfe, J. L. (1966). *How to raise an emotionally healthy, happy child*. The Institute for Rational Living.
43. Barrish, I. J., & Barrish, H. H. (1983). *Managing parental anger*. Overland Press.
44. Barrish, I. J., & Barrish, H. H. (1985). *Surviving and enjoying your adolescent*. Westport Publishers.
45. Barrish, I. J., & Barrish, H. H. (1989). *Surviving and enjoying your adolescent*. Westport Publishers.
46. Hauck, P. (1983). Working with parents. In A. Ellis & M. E. Bernard (Eds.), *Rational-emotive approaches to the problems of childhood* (pp. 333–366). Plenum Press.
47. Bernard, M. E., & Joyce, M. R. (1984). *Rational-emotive therapy with children and adolescents: Theory, treatment strategies, preventative methods*. Wiley.
48. Vernon, A. (2002). *What works when with children and adolescents: A handbook of individual counseling techniques*. Research Press.
49. Vernon, A. (2009). *More what works when with children and adolescents: A handbook of individual counseling techniques*. Research Press.
50. Weinrach, S., DiGiuseppe, R., Wolfe, J., Ellis, A., Bernard, M. E., Dryden, W., et al. (2006). Rational emotive behavior therapy after Ellis: Predictions for the future. *Journal of Rational-Emotive Cognitive-Behavior Therapy*, *24*(4), 199–215.
51. Dryden, W., Hurton, N., Malki, D., Manias, P., & Wiiliams, K. (2008). Patients' doubts, reservations and objections to the ABC's of REBT and their application. *Journal of Rational-Emotive & Cognitive-Behavior Therapy*, *26*, 63–88.
52. Beara, V. (2015). The contribution of REBT in addressing the givens of existence. *Journal of Rational-Emotive & Cognitive-Behavior Therapy*. https://doi.org/10.1007/s10942-015-0209-8
53. David, D., Szentagotai, A., Eva, K., & Macavei, B. (2005). A synopsis of rational-emotive behavior therapy (REBT); fundamental and applied research. *Journal of Rational-Emotive & Cognitive-Behavior Therapy*. https://doi.org/10.1007/s10942-005-0011-0
54. Weinrach, S. G. (2006). Rational emotive behavior therapy: A tough-minded therapy for a tender-minded profession. *Journal of Rational-Emotive & Cognitive-Behavior Therapy*. https://doi.org/10.1007/s10942-006-0043-0
55. Weinrach, S. G., Ellis, A., DiGiuseppe, R., Bernard, M. E., Dryden, W., Kassinove, H., Morris, G. B., Vernon, A., & Wolfe, J. (2006). Rational emotive behavior therapy after Ellis: Predictions for the future. *Journal of Rational-Emotive & Cognitive-Behavior Therapy*. https://doi.org/10.1007/s10942-006-0045-y
56. Dryden, W. (2011). Albert Ellis and rational emotive behavior therapy: A personal reflection. *Journal of Rational-Emotive & Cognitive-Behavior Therapy*. https://doi.org/10.1007/s10942-011-0143-3
57. Neenan, M. (2001). REBT 45 years on: Still on the sidelines. Journal of Rational-Emotive & Cognitive-Behavior Therapy. https://doi.org/10.1023/a:1007843232639
58. Vernon, A. (2011). Rational emotive behavior therapy: The past, present, and future. *Journal of Rational-Emotive & Cognitive-Behavior Therapy*. https://doi.org/10.1007/s10942-011-0147-z
59. Ziegler, D. J. (2000). Basic assumptions concerning human nature underlying rational emotive behavior therapy (REBT) personality theory. *Journal of Rational-Emotive & Cognitive-Behavior Therapy*. https://doi.org/10.1023/a:1007858502932
60. Dryden, W. (2011). The "ABCs" of REBT I: A preliminary study of errors and confusions in counselling and psychotherapy textbooks. *Journal of Rational-Emotive & Cognitive-Behavior Therapy*. https://doi.org/10.1007/s10942-011-0137-1

Chapter 2
Beliefs

Introduction by the Editor

Chapter Two focuses on the construct of beliefs as the psychological core of Rational Emotive Behavior Therapy. While the previous chapter established the theoretical and empirical foundations of REBT, the present chapter moves more deeply into the structure, function, development, and impact of beliefs themselves. Within REBT, beliefs are not treated as peripheral cognitive events but as central evaluative processes that shape emotional experience, behavioral responses, and long term psychological adjustment. The collection of papers included in this chapter was selected to provide a comprehensive examination of beliefs across developmental stages, clinical populations, and applied contexts. Together, they advance the understanding of how beliefs operate, how they are measured, how they contribute to psychopathology, and how they may be modified through therapeutic intervention.

The topic of this chapter is therefore the multidimensional study of beliefs within the REBT framework. This includes irrational and rational beliefs, demandingness, catastrophizing, frustration intolerance, global evaluations of self and others, as well as adaptive alternatives grounded in flexibility and acceptance. The selected research examines beliefs in children, adolescents, and adults, explores their relationship to emotional disorders including anxiety, depression, and eating pathology, and evaluates how belief structures interact with vulnerability factors and protective processes. By focusing on beliefs as the primary mediating mechanism between life events and emotional outcomes, this chapter highlights the conceptual precision and explanatory power of the REBT model.

These particular papers were included because they collectively represent a broad and contemporary examination of beliefs. Some investigate belief structures in youth populations, which is critical for understanding how irrational patterns emerge early and become consolidated over time. Others examine beliefs in relation to specific clinical presentations such as eating disorders, mood disturbances, and performance related stress. Several studies explore

M. Siddique et al., *Rational Emotive Behavior Therapy*,
https://doi.org/10.1007/978-3-032-32191-6_2

psychometric validation and conceptual clarification, ensuring that belief constructs are rigorously defined and empirically measurable. Additional contributions examine the predictive power of beliefs, their transdiagnostic relevance, and their responsiveness to intervention. By bringing these works together, the chapter provides a layered understanding of beliefs as both developmental phenomena and active determinants of psychological health.

Readers will learn how beliefs function as evaluative filters through which individuals interpret their experiences. Within REBT, beliefs are not limited to automatic thoughts but reflect deeper philosophical commitments about self, others, and the world. Irrational beliefs are characterized by rigidity, absolutism, and overgeneralized evaluation. They often take the form of internal demands, such as the insistence that one must perform perfectly, must be approved by others, or must not encounter discomfort. These demands frequently give rise to secondary processes including catastrophizing, which involves exaggerating the negative consequences of events; frustration intolerance, which reflects difficulty accepting discomfort or delay; and global rating of worth, in which individuals define themselves or others in totalizing terms based on limited evidence.

Across the studies included in this chapter, a consistent finding is that irrational beliefs significantly predict psychological distress across age groups. In youth populations, irrational beliefs are associated with heightened vulnerability to anxiety, depressive symptoms, and behavioral difficulties. The developmental perspective offered by several of these papers demonstrates that rigid evaluative thinking can be identified early, suggesting that belief based interventions may serve a preventative function. These findings underscore the importance of addressing beliefs not only in adult psychotherapy but also in school based and early intervention settings.

In adult populations, irrational beliefs continue to demonstrate strong associations with emotional disorders. Research examining eating pathology, for example, indicates that rigid demands related to body image, perfectionism, and approval seeking are linked to maladaptive eating behaviors and cognitive distortions about weight and self worth. These findings support the transdiagnostic applicability of REBT by demonstrating that core belief structures operate across different symptom domains. Similarly, studies examining mood and anxiety disorders reveal that demandingness and catastrophizing remain central cognitive predictors of emotional disturbance.

Another important theme emerging from this body of research is the distinction between irrational and rational beliefs. Rational beliefs are characterized by flexibility, preference rather than demand, and unconditional acceptance of self and others. The empirical findings indicate that rational beliefs are not merely the absence of irrationality but represent distinct and measurable constructs associated with resilience, adaptive coping, and psychological wellbeing. This distinction strengthens the theoretical claim that emotional health is not achieved by eliminating negative experience but by transforming rigid evaluative systems into flexible and reality based philosophies.

Several of the selected papers contribute to the ongoing refinement of measurement tools designed to assess belief structures. Factor analytic studies support the multidimensional nature of irrational beliefs, while also confirming the centrality of demandingness as a foundational component. The research suggests that demandingness often functions as a primary cognitive process that activates secondary processes such as catastrophizing and frustration intolerance. This hierarchical structure enhances conceptual clarity and provides direction for targeted intervention strategies. Reliable measurement is essential for advancing both research and clinical practice, and these contributions significantly strengthen the empirical base of belief assessment.

The chapter also addresses the interaction between beliefs and contextual stressors. Although external events may trigger emotional responses, the research consistently demonstrates that beliefs mediate the intensity and duration of those responses. This mediation model is evident across different populations and problem areas. Whether examining academic stress in adolescents, body dissatisfaction in young adults, or broader emotional adjustment, beliefs emerge as the explanatory link between situational challenges and psychological outcomes. Such findings reinforce the central REBT proposition that cognition plays a determining role in emotional disturbance.

An additional contribution of these studies lies in their exploration of belief modification through intervention. Several papers examine the impact of cognitive restructuring strategies grounded in REBT principles. The findings suggest that targeted disputation of irrational beliefs leads to measurable reductions in emotional distress and maladaptive behavior. Importantly, change in belief structure often precedes and predicts improvement in emotional outcomes, supporting the causal status of beliefs within the therapeutic process. This evidence strengthens the theoretical integrity of REBT by demonstrating alignment between conceptual assumptions and observed clinical change.

Despite the substantial empirical support, the research also highlights areas in need of further exploration. Longitudinal studies remain relatively limited, and greater attention to the stability and evolution of beliefs over time would enhance developmental understanding. Cultural diversity in samples also warrants expansion. While belief constructs appear robust across studied populations, more cross cultural research is needed to examine how sociocultural factors shape the expression and content of irrational and rational beliefs. Furthermore, integration with emerging constructs such as metacognition and emotional regulation strategies may provide additional insight into the complexity of belief systems.

Another gap concerns the differentiation between related cognitive constructs. Although irrational beliefs overlap conceptually with maladaptive schemas and cognitive distortions, clearer empirical comparisons would strengthen theoretical precision. Research that directly contrasts REBT belief constructs with schema based models or other cognitive frameworks would help delineate unique contributions and potential areas of integration. Such comparative studies would not diminish the distinctiveness of REBT but would situate it more clearly within the broader cognitive behavioral landscape.

In reviewing these studies collectively, several overarching findings emerge. First, beliefs are measurable, multidimensional, and empirically valid constructs. Second, irrational beliefs consistently predict emotional and behavioral disturbance across age groups and clinical contexts. Third, rational beliefs are independently associated with resilience and adaptive functioning. Fourth, modification of irrational beliefs through structured intervention leads to meaningful psychological improvement. These conclusions reinforce the theoretical centrality of beliefs within REBT and affirm their relevance to both research and applied practice.

The chapter also provides insight into the philosophical depth of belief based intervention. REBT does not merely challenge surface level thoughts but encourages individuals to examine and revise deeply held evaluative principles. This philosophical component distinguishes belief work within REBT from more superficial cognitive restructuring approaches. By promoting unconditional self acceptance, tolerance of discomfort, and flexible goal pursuit, REBT addresses not only symptom reduction but broader life philosophy. The research reviewed here demonstrates that such philosophical shifts are associated with tangible emotional benefits.

A notable observation arising from synthesis of these papers is the developmental continuity of belief processes. Irrational beliefs identified in childhood often resemble those observed in adulthood, suggesting that early cognitive patterns may persist unless actively addressed. This continuity underscores the importance of preventative interventions and psychoeducational efforts aimed at fostering rational belief systems early in life. It also suggests that belief modification may have long term protective effects against the recurrence of emotional disturbance.

Readers will therefore gain a detailed understanding of beliefs as the central mechanism of change within REBT. They will see how beliefs are structured, how they influence emotion and behavior, how they are measured, and how they can be modified. They will also recognize that belief systems are not static but responsive to intervention, context, and developmental influences. The integration of empirical findings across diverse populations enhances confidence in the generalizability of these conclusions.

The main takeaways from this chapter can be summarized in several key points. Beliefs represent the evaluative core of emotional experience. Irrational beliefs are characterized by rigidity and absolutism and are strongly associated with psychological distress. Rational beliefs reflect flexibility and acceptance and are linked to resilience. Measurement tools for assessing belief structures have advanced significantly, strengthening the scientific credibility of the REBT model. Intervention strategies targeting belief modification produce measurable and meaningful improvement. At the same time, ongoing research is needed to expand longitudinal, cultural, and comparative perspectives.

In conclusion, this chapter deepens the examination of beliefs as the defining feature of Rational Emotive Behavior Therapy. By assembling contemporary research that spans developmental stages, clinical domains, and methodological approaches, it demonstrates that beliefs are not abstract philosophical constructs but empirically grounded determinants of psychological functioning. The studies included here collectively affirm that belief systems shape emotional reality and that intentional modification of those systems offers a powerful pathway to psychological health. As the book progresses, this emphasis on beliefs will continue to serve as a unifying thread, linking theory, research, and applied practice within the REBT tradition.

Machine Generated Summaries

Disclaimer: The summaries in this chapter were generated from Springer Nature publications using extractive AI auto-summarization: An extraction-based summarizer aims to identify the most important sentences of a text using an algorithm and uses those original sentences to create the auto-summary (unlike generative AI). As the constituted sentences are machine selected, they may not fully reflect the body of the work, so we strongly advise that the original content is read and cited. The auto generated summaries were curated by the editor to meet Springer Nature publication standards. To cite this content, please refer to the original papers.

Machine generated keywords: student, child, item, ab, rbs, ibs, child adolescent, adolescent, irrational belief, college, irrational, career, selfesteem, eat, low frustration

Disputing Irrational Beliefs Among Convicted Terrorists and Extremist Beliefs [119]

This is a machine-generated summary of:

Aldahadha, Basim: Disputing Irrational Beliefs Among Convicted Terrorists and Extremist Beliefs [119]

Published in: Journal of Rational-Emotive & Cognitive-Behavior Therapy (2018)

Link to original: https://doi.org/10.1007/s10942-018-0293-7

If you want to cite the papers, please refer to the original.

For technical reasons we could not place the page where the original quote is coming from.

Research Highlights

Irrational beliefs are associated with dysfunctional emotions and behaviors, such as heightened anxiety, feelings of anger, and maladaptive behaviors like social avoidance and aggression. The goal of Rational Emotive Behavior Therapy (REBT) is to help individuals change irrational beliefs to rational ones, promoting psychological well-being. However, while REBT has been extensively used for personal issues, its application to socio-political extremism remains underexplored. Now a new study by Basim Aldahadha and colleagues investigates the effectiveness of a Disputing Irrational Beliefs Program (DIBP) in reducing irrational beliefs among terrorist and extremist prisoners in Jordan.

The study involved a quasi-experimental design with an experimental group (EG) and a control group (CG) of prisoners from Bab Al-Hawa, Al-Juwaideh, and Swaqa prisons. Participants were assessed using the Irrational Beliefs Scale (IBS), which was translated into Arabic and validated for this context. The DIBP consisted of 12 weekly sessions focusing on disputing irrational beliefs through logical, empirical, functional, and rational alternative strategies. According to Aldahadha, "The program aimed to help members recognize the most common irrational beliefs and train them on practicing social support network exercises." Pre- and post-test scores on the IBS were compared to evaluate the program's effectiveness.

The results showed that the EG had significantly more positive effects and less negative effects compared to the CG at the end of the study. Extremists showed a more substantial decrease in IBS scores than terrorists, indicating that they responded better to the DIBP interventions. Aldahadha notes, "It is clear that members of the study sample held unrealistic and arbitrary ideas." This study highlights the potential of REBT-based interventions in reducing irrational beliefs among extremists and terrorists. Future research should explore other cognitive strategies and emphasize the importance of continuous psychological services in prisons to foster rational thinking and prosocial behavior.

A rational emotive behavior therapy-based intervention for binge eating behavior management among female students: A quasi-experimental study [120]

This is a machine-generated summary of:

Yang, Jiwon; Han, Kuem Sun: A rational emotive behavior therapy-based intervention for binge eating behavior management among female students: a quasi-experimental study [120]

Published in: Journal of Eating Disorders (2020)

Link to original: https://doi.org/10.1186/s40337-020-00347-8

If you want to cite the papers, please refer to the original.

For technical reasons we could not place the page where the original quote is coming from.

Research Highlights

Over the past two decades, South Korean society has increasingly pursued values based on physical appearance, leading to distorted body images and dissatisfaction among women, particularly college students. This has resulted in inappropriate eating habits and a high likelihood of developing eating disorders. Now a new study by Jiwon Yang and colleagues from Sun Moon University addresses binge eating behavior and related factors among female college students in Korea, aiming to prevent the development of eating disorders through an intervention based on rational emotive behavior therapy (REBT).

The study employed a quasi-experimental design with a nonequivalent control group pretest-posttest approach. Participants were recruited from S University in C city and were divided into experimental and control groups. The experimental group attended eight REBT sessions over four weeks, focusing on cognitive restructuring, emotional control, and behavioral modification. The program included activities such as identifying belief systems, emotional expression, and problem-solving skills training. Participants also maintained dietary diaries to monitor their eating habits. The control group received a single session on binge eating education. Data were collected using structured questionnaires assessing self-esteem, covert narcissism, perfectionism, body dissatisfaction, anxiety, depression, and binge eating before and after the intervention.

The REBT-based program demonstrated significant positive effects on participants' self-esteem while reducing covert narcissism, body dissatisfaction, anxiety, depression, and binge eating behaviors. Yang notes that "the integrative cognitive, emotional, and behavioral techniques of REBT are appropriate and useful for intervention in binge eating behavior." However, the study's limitations include its focus on female students from one university and the need for long-term follow-up to verify sustained effects. Future research should expand the target population and explore alternative delivery methods such as social media or mobile applications to increase accessibility.

Changes in irrational beliefs are responsible for the efficacy of the REThink therapeutic game in preventing emotional disorders in children and adolescents: mechanisms of change analysis of a randomized clinical trial [121]

This is a machine-generated summary of:

David, Oana A.; Cardoş, Roxana A. I.; Matu, Silviu: Changes in irrational beliefs are responsible for the efficacy of the REThink therapeutic game in preventing emotional disorders in children and adolescents: mechanisms of change analysis of a randomized clinical trial [121]

Published in: European Child & Adolescent Psychiatry (2018)

Link to original: https://doi.org/10.1007/s00787-018-1195-z

If you want to cite the papers, please refer to the original.

For technical reasons we could not place the page where the original quote is coming from.

Research Highlights

Despite the alarming prevalence of childhood mental disorders and the accompanying personal, economic, and social costs, the focus in mental health has been primarily on treatment rather than prevention. Developing effective prevention strategies for children and adolescents is crucial to reduce the prevalence and impact of mental health disorders. Now a new study by Oana A. David and colleagues introduces RET hink, an online therapeutic game designed to promote emotional resilience in undiagnosed children and adolescents.

The study involved 150 healthy children and adolescents aged between 10 and 14 years, recruited from one middle school and one high school. Participants were randomly assigned to three groups: a waitlist control group, a Rational-Emotive Behavioral Education (REBE) group, and the RET hink intervention group. The RET hink game features a character named RETMAN who helps players develop rational thinking skills through various levels that address different cognitive-behavioral concepts such as identifying emotions, changing irrational beliefs, problem-solving, relaxation techniques, and building happiness skills. The intervention was delivered over seven weeks with pre-intervention, intermediate, and post-intervention assessments using standardized questionnaires to measure emotional symptoms, depressive mood, irrational beliefs, and automatic thoughts.

The results indicated that the RET hink intervention significantly decreased emotional symptoms and depressive mood compared to the control groups. The study found that changes in irrational beliefs mediated these improvements, supporting the theoretical model of Rational Emotive Behavioral Therapy (REBT).

"Our findings suggest that targeting core dysfunctional beliefs directly through an engaging medium like a video game can be an effective strategy for preventing emotional difficulties in youth," says David. Future research should explore the long-term effects of such interventions and their applicability in diverse settings to further validate these promising findings.

The Development of a Short Form of an Irrational/Rational Beliefs Scale [122]

This is a machine-generated summary of:

DiGiuseppe, Raymond; Gorman, Bernard; Raptis, Joanne; Agiurgioaei-Boie, Alina; Agiurgioaei, Fabian; Leaf, Russell; Robin, Mitchell W.: The Development of a Short Form of an Irrational/Rational Beliefs Scale [122]

Published in: Journal of Rational-Emotive & Cognitive-Behavior Therapy (2021)

Link to original: https://doi.org/10.1007/s10942-021-00386-3

If you want to cite the papers, please refer to the original.

For technical reasons we could not place the page where the original quote is coming from.

Research Highlights

Ellis's Rational Emotive Behavior Therapy (REBT) is a well-established form of cognitive-behavior therapy that focuses on identifying and altering irrational beliefs (IBs) to alleviate emotional and behavioral disturbances. Despite its prominence, REBT's scientific progress has been limited by the lack of concise and valid measures to assess its core constructs. Now, a new study by Raymond DiGiuseppe and colleagues addresses this gap by developing a short form of the Attitudes and Belief Scale-2 (ABS-2), aiming to provide a more practical tool for both research and clinical use.

DiGiuseppe et al. selected items for the ABS-2 Short Form (ABS-2-SF) based on their correlation with total parcel scores, ability to distinguish between clinical and non-clinical groups, and their relationship with measures of psychological disturbance. The study involved confirmatory factor analysis (CFA) using data from diverse samples, including psychotherapy clients, college students, and substance abuse rehabilitation residents. The researchers tested several models to determine the best fit for the ABS-2-SF's factor structure. They found that an eight-factor model representing four irrational and four rational cognitive processes provided the best fit, supporting REBT theory that each irrational belief has a corresponding rational alternative.

The ABS-2-SF demonstrated excellent internal consistency and validity, with significant correlations with measures of psychopathology such as the Outcomes Questionnaire (OQ) and the Psychiatric Disorders Screening Questionnaire (PDSQ). The study's findings suggest that the ABS-2-SF can effectively measure IBs and RBs across different content domains—achievement, affiliation, and comfort—providing valuable insights into general irrationality and rationality. Future research could explore using the ABS-2-SF to test hypotheses about specific cognitive processes or content domains related to various psychological disturbances, thereby advancing our understanding of REBT's mechanisms of change. As DiGiuseppe notes, "The ease of administering the ABS-2-SF allows for more frequent data collection in clinical settings, facilitating studies on the process of change in REBT."

Exploring the Role of Irrational Beliefs, Lifestyle Behaviors, and Educational Status in 10-Year Cardiovascular Disease Risk: the ATTICA Epidemiological Study [123]

This is a machine-generated summary of:

Vassou, Christina; Georgousopoulou, Ekavi N.; Yannakoulia, Mary; Chrysohoou, Christina; Papageorgiou, Charalabos; Pitsavos, Christos; Cropley, Mark; Panagiotakos, Demosthenes B.: Exploring the Role of Irrational Beliefs, Lifestyle Behaviors, and Educational Status in 10-Year Cardiovascular Disease Risk: the ATTICA Epidemiological Study [123]

Published in: International Journal of Behavioral Medicine (2022)

Link to original: https://doi.org/10.1007/s12529-022-10091-9

If you want to cite the papers, please refer to the original.

For technical reasons we could not place the page where the original quote is coming from.

Research Highlights
Cardiovascular diseases (CVD) are the leading cause of morbidity and mortality worldwide, with over 75% of CVD deaths occurring in low- and middle-income countries, according to the World Health Organization. While biological, behavioral, and social risk factors for CVD are well-documented, the role of psychological factors, particularly irrational beliefs, in the pathogenesis of CVD remains under-explored. Now a new study by Christina Vassou and colleagues investigates the association between irrational beliefs and CVD risk over a 10-year period, considering socioeconomic indicators, lifestyle behaviors, and psychological disturbances.

The ATTICA study is a population-based prospective survey conducted in Greece from 2001 to 2012. Researchers recruited 3,042 adults who provided blood samples and sociodemographic, lifestyle, and medical information. A subsample of 853 participants underwent psychological evaluation using the Irrational Beliefs Inventory (IBI), Zung Self-Rating Depression Scale (ZDRS), and State Anxiety subscale of the Spielberger State-Trait Anxiety Inventory (STAI). Over a decade-long follow-up, the incidence of CVD events was recorded. The study found that higher IBI scores were significantly associated with increased CVD risk even after adjusting for confounders such as age, sex, smoking habits, physical activity status, dietary habits, hypertension, diabetes, and hypercholesterolemia.

This study highlights that irrational beliefs are a significant predictor of long-term CVD risk. Vassou et al. suggest that educational status plays a moderating role in this relationship; individuals with lower education levels exhibited stronger associations between irrational beliefs and CVD risk. The findings underscore the importance of addressing psychological factors in CVD prevention strategies. Future research should explore interventions targeting irrational beliefs to mitigate their impact on cardiovascular health. As Vassou notes, "Detection of patients with high endorsement of irrational beliefs can be accomplished by administering negative beliefs questionnaires in public and private health care services as part of primary prevention."

The Effect of Rational Emotive Behavior Therapy on Irrational Career Beliefs of Students of Electrical Electronics and Other Engineering Trades in Technical Colleges in Nigeria [124]

This is a machine-generated summary of:

Ogbuanya, Theresa Chinyere; Eseadi, Chiedu; Orji, Chibueze Tobias; Anyanwu, Joy I.; Joachim, Omeje C.; Otu, Mkpoikanke S.: The Effect of Rational Emotive Behavior Therapy on Irrational Career Beliefs of Students of Electrical Electronics and Other Engineering Trades in Technical Colleges in Nigeria [124]

Published in: Journal of Rational-Emotive & Cognitive-Behavior Therapy (2017)

Link to original: https://doi.org/10.1007/s10942-017-0282-2

If you want to cite the papers, please refer to the original.

For technical reasons we could not place the page where the original quote is coming from.

Research Highlights

The need to explore clients' career beliefs has received increased attention in career counseling literature, as ignoring these beliefs can diminish the impact of career counseling programs. Career beliefs, particularly irrational ones, can significantly influence career-related outcomes such as job satisfaction and career decision-making. Now, a new study by Theresa Chinyere Ogbuanya and colleagues examines the effectiveness of a Rational Emotive Behavior Therapy (REBT) career program on irrational career beliefs among students in technical colleges in Nigeria.

Ogbuanya et al. conducted a study involving first-year students from technical colleges in Southeast Nigeria, who were at a critical stage of choosing their trade specialization. The researchers employed a pretest-posttest control group design, with participants randomly assigned to either an REBT treatment group or a waitlist control group. The REBT program consisted of twenty 45-minute sessions over ten weeks, focusing on identifying, challenging, and modifying irrational career beliefs using the ABCDE model of REBT. Data were collected at four time points: pretest, posttest, three-month follow-up, and six-month follow-up. The Career Beliefs Inventory (CBI) and Career Belief Patterns Scale (CBPS-2) were used to measure the participants' irrational career beliefs.

The study found that participants in the REBT treatment group showed a significant reduction in irrational career beliefs compared to those in the waitlist control group at posttest and follow-up evaluations. According to Ogbuanya, "The significant reduction in irrational career beliefs was maintained at both three- and six-month follow-ups." This suggests that the REBT program effectively helped students develop more rational career beliefs, which could lead to better career decision-making. Future research should explore the impact of REBT-based interventions on other career-related outcomes such as job satisfaction and organizational commitment. Additionally, examining how these interventions can reduce career choice anxiety and improve self-efficacy among diverse student populations would be valuable.

Teacher Beliefs and Stress [125]

This is a machine-generated summary of:

Bernard, Michael E.: Teacher Beliefs and Stress [125]

Published in: Journal of Rational-Emotive & Cognitive-Behavior Therapy (2016)

Link to original: https://doi.org/10.1007/s10942-016-0238-y

If you want to cite the papers, please refer to the original.

For technical reasons we could not place the page where the original quote is coming from.

Research Highlights

Over the past two decades, the number of studies on occupational stress in the teaching profession has dramatically increased, reflecting growing international concern with this topic. Studies indicate that approximately 30–40% of teachers show some stress symptoms, and about 20–25% of them have burnout symptoms. When compared with other professions, teachers report one of the highest levels of occupational stress. Now a new study by Michael E. Bernard and colleagues investigates the role of irrational beliefs in mediating teacher stress and burnout.

The study utilized the Teacher Irrational Belief Scale (TIBS) to measure irrational beliefs among teachers in Victoria, Australia. Questionnaires were distributed to teachers at the beginning of a curriculum in-service day, and responses were collected from 300 participants. The TIBS assessed four types of irrational beliefs: absolutizing, awfulizing, low frustration tolerance, and global rating. The researchers also measured teacher stress using a single-question format that asked teachers to rate the stressfulness of various teaching-related problems on a five-point scale. Factor analysis revealed four principal factors: Self-downing, Authoritarianism, Demands for Justice, and Low Frustration Tolerance. The study found significant correlations between these irrational beliefs and different types of teacher stress.

The findings suggest that more experienced teachers tend to endorse fewer irrational beliefs than their less experienced counterparts. This could be due to either a natural maturation process or the early departure of more stress-prone individuals from the profession. Bernard notes that "the tendency to take bad things personally and blow time and workload pressures out of proportion mediates high levels of stress." Future research should explore whether these findings hold true across different cultural contexts and employ additional data collection methods such as interviews or behavioral ratings to further validate the relationship between irrational beliefs and teacher stress.

Evaluation of the Psychometric Properties of a Measure of Child Irrationality [126]

This is a machine-generated summary of:

Terjesen, Mark D.; Kassay, Kimberly S.; Anderson, Dana L.: Evaluation of the Psychometric Properties of a Measure of Child Irrationality [126]

Published in: Journal of Rational-Emotive & Cognitive-Behavior Therapy (2017)

Link to original: https://doi.org/10.1007/s10942-017-0269-z

If you want to cite the papers, please refer to the original.

For technical reasons we could not place the page where the original quote is coming from.

Research Highlights

Cognitive behavioral therapy (CBT) is a widely used form of psychotherapy that aims to create lasting changes in clients by focusing on the interplay between cognitive activity and behavior. Rational-Emotive Behavior Therapy (REBT), a type of CBT developed by Albert Ellis, has been particularly effective in treating various emotional and behavioral issues in children and adolescents. Despite its success, there is a need for reliable measures to assess irrational beliefs in youth, which are central to REBT's theoretical framework. Now, a new study by Mark D. Terjesen and colleagues seeks to validate the Child and Adolescent Scale of Irrationality (CASI) to better understand its psychometric properties and utility in clinical settings.

The study involved two main investigations: the first examined the psychometric properties and factor structure of the CASI using data from various populations, while the second aimed to validate the CASI by comparing it with a well-established measure of social-emotional functioning, the Behavior Assessment System for Children Second Edition Self Report of Personality Form (BASC-2 SRP). The researchers consulted eight REBT experts to rate each CASI item according to specific irrational beliefs proposed by Ellis. Data were collected from adolescents across different settings, including urban high schools and outpatient mental health clinics. The study found that while the CASI demonstrated high internal reliability as a whole, there was variability in the reliability of specific irrational belief scales.

The findings suggest that children's thought patterns may not align neatly with specific domains of irrational beliefs as seen in adults. This raises questions about whether it is more useful to consider overall irrationality rather than specific belief patterns when assessing emotional and behavioral difficulties in youth. "The strong correlations between the CASI and measures of social-emotional functioning provide evidence of validity," says Terjesen. Future research should focus on revising the CASI to reflect current vernacular and concerns, as well as exploring how irrational beliefs change with age and differ by gender. A reliable measure could significantly enhance clinical practice by helping practitioners target specific beliefs for change, thereby supporting REBT's theoretical framework.

The Development of a Measure of Irrational/Rational Beliefs [127]

This is a machine-generated summary of:

DiGiuseppe, Raymond; Leaf, Russell; Gorman, Bernard; Robin, Mitchell W.: The Development of a Measure of Irrational/Rational Beliefs [127]

Published in: Journal of Rational-Emotive & Cognitive-Behavior Therapy (2017)

Link to original: https://doi.org/10.1007/s10942-017-0273-3

If you want to cite the papers, please refer to the original.

For technical reasons we could not place the page where the original quote is coming from.

Research Highlights

The Attitudes and Belief Scale (ABS) measures Ellis' Irrational and Rational Beliefs, a core component of Rational Emotive Behavior Therapy (REBT). Although DiGiuseppe and colleagues developed the ABS, this represents the first publication on its development and psychometric properties. Now, a new study by Raymond DiGiuseppe and colleagues discusses the development of the ABS, compares it with other measures of irrational beliefs, and presents its psychometric properties.

The study involved constructing ABS items based on Burgess' original measure but with improvements such as using only self-referentially worded items and more specific content items. The authors created rational items that were complex sentences representing the antitheses of irrational beliefs. For example, an irrational item reflecting Demandingness was "I must be liked by people who are important to me," while the corresponding rational item was "I want to be liked by people who are important to me, but I realize I do not have to be liked by them." The ABS consists of items fitting into a 4x3x2 matrix: four cognitive processes (Demandingness, Self-Downing, Frustration Intolerance, Awfulizing), three content areas (Affiliation, Achievement, Comfort), and two types of wording (irrational and rational).

The study found that the ABS has excellent internal consistency and correlates well with measures of psychological disturbance. However, it failed to support Ellis' hypothesis on the centrality of Demandingness as the core irrational belief. The findings suggest that rationally worded items were more effective at discriminating between non-clinical and clinical groups than irrationally worded items. Future research should focus on refining the scale's factor structure and exploring its applicability across different cultural contexts. As DiGiuseppe notes, "REBT research has focused too much on the irrational side of human nature and not enough on the alternative rational side."

The Role of Catastrophizing Beliefs in Effective Chronic Pain Treatment [128]

This is a machine-generated summary of:

Smith, Katie; Herman, Michael; Smith, Christopher: The Role of Catastrophizing Beliefs in Effective Chronic Pain Treatment [128]

Published in: Journal of Rational-Emotive & Cognitive-Behavior Therapy (2015)

Link to original: https://doi.org/10.1007/s10942-015-0220-0

If you want to cite the papers, please refer to the original.

For technical reasons we could not place the page where the original quote is coming from.

Research Highlights

The Role of Catastrophizing Beliefs in Effective Chronic Pain Treatment

Discussing effective treatment of pain requires an understanding of the context that informs pain management goals and goal setting. In mainstream health care and mental health practice, goals are often set around what is considered "normal" for a healthy individual to experience. One of the many problems in the pursuit of a pain management model is a result of the ongoing revisions to the definition of normal. Now, a new study by Katie Smith and colleagues explores how catastrophizing beliefs impact chronic pain treatment and suggests new directions for more effective management.

Smith and her team conducted a comprehensive review of existing literature on cognitive approaches to chronic pain, focusing on how catastrophizing beliefs—irrationally negative evaluations of pain—affect patient outcomes. The researchers utilized a biopsychosocial framework to assess the interplay between cognitive appraisals, emotional responses, and physical sensations. "Catastrophizing dramatically inhibits the ability to keep up with daily activities," Smith notes, emphasizing that this cognitive style exacerbates pain perception and disability. The study involved analyzing various cognitive-behavioral therapy (CBT) modalities, including Rational Emotive Behavior Therapy (REBT) and Acceptance and Commitment Therapy (ACT), which target maladaptive appraisals to improve patient functioning.

The main advance from Smith's research is the identification of specific cognitive interventions that can mitigate the negative impact of catastrophizing on chronic pain patients. By promoting cognitive flexibility and unconditional acceptance, REBT and ACT offer promising avenues for treatment. "Effective treatment needs to focus on how the patient experiences their immediate context via their own cognitive evaluations," Smith concludes. Future research should explore broader accessibility to these interventions, potentially through telemedicine or group therapy settings, to enhance their reach and efficacy in managing chronic pain.

A Turkish Translation of a Measure of Irrational and Rational Beliefs: Reliability, Validity Studies and Confirmation of the Four Cognitive Processes Model [129]

This is a machine-generated summary of:

Artiran, Murat; DiGiuseppe, Raymond: A Turkish Translation of a Measure of Irrational and Rational Beliefs: Reliability, Validity Studies and Confirmation of the Four Cognitive Processes Model [129]

Published in: Journal of Rational-Emotive & Cognitive-Behavior Therapy (2020)

Link to original: https://doi.org/10.1007/s10942-020-00340-9

If you want to cite the papers, please refer to the original.

For technical reasons we could not place the page where the original quote is coming from.

Research Highlights

Albert Ellis's Rational Emotive Behavior Therapy (REBT) posits that irrational beliefs (IBs) are central to emotional disturbances, while rational beliefs (RBs) foster healthier emotional responses. Despite the widespread use of REBT, most measures of IBs and RBs are rooted in Western cultural contexts, raising questions about their applicability in non-Western cultures. Now, a new study by Murat Artiran and colleagues has translated and validated the Attitudes and Beliefs Scale-2 (ABS-2) into Turkish to assess its reliability and validity within a Turkish cultural context.

The study involved a meticulous translation process, including forward and backward translations by bilingual scholars, followed by pilot testing with Turkish university students to ensure clarity and cultural relevance. The researchers then administered both the English and Turkish versions of the ABS-2 to bilingual participants to confirm that the translations were equivalent. The study also included test-retest reliability assessments with a sample from Istanbul, demonstrating high internal consistency for both IB and RB subscales. Furthermore, exploratory factor analysis (EFA) and confirmatory factor analysis (CFA) were conducted to examine the scale's factor structure, revealing that separating IBs and RBs into distinct scales provided the best fit.

This research represents a significant advance in cross-cultural psychology by providing a validated tool for assessing REBT constructs in Turkey. "Our findings support the use of the ABS-2 in non-Western cultures," says Artiran. Future research should explore the scale's applicability in clinical populations and other non-Western contexts. Additionally, investigating whether challenging IBs or promoting RBs is more effective in therapy could provide deeper insights into the mechanisms of change in REBT. This study lays the groundwork for such investigations, contributing to a more global understanding of cognitive-behavioral therapies.

Assessing the Efficacy of Rational Emotive Behavior Intervention for Visually Impaired Upper Basic School Children with Negative Self-belief/Personal Value System [130]

This is a machine-generated summary of:

Ede, Moses Onyemaechi; Okeke, Chinedu Ifedi; Chukwu, Chinyere Loveth: Assessing the Efficacy of Rational Emotive Behavior Intervention for Visually Impaired Upper Basic School Children with Negative Self-belief/Personal Value System [130]

Published in: Journal of Rational-Emotive & Cognitive-Behavior Therapy (2021)

Link to original: https://doi.org/10.1007/s10942-021-00419-x

If you want to cite the papers, please refer to the original.

For technical reasons we could not place the page where the original quote is coming from.

Research Highlights

Values are established enduring beliefs about the worth of certain behaviors and things, significantly influencing an individual's actions and experiences. For students, these values can affect school engagement, social relationships, and emotional reactions. However, students living with blindness (SLB) in Nigeria often develop a Negative Personal Value System (NPVS) due to hostile environments and unsupportive school systems. Now a new study by Moses Onyemaechi Ede and colleagues suggests that Rational Emotive Behavior Therapy (REBT) could effectively reduce NPVS among SLB.

The study employed a randomized controlled trial design involving primary school children living with blindness in Enugu State, Nigeria. Participants were divided into a treatment group, which received a value-based REBT program, and a no-contact control group. The REBT program aimed to correct irrational beliefs associated with NPVS through cognitive disputation, behavioral exercises, and other therapeutic strategies over 12 weeks. "We hypothesized that NPVS or self-disbeliefs would be significantly reduced when exposed to the REBT-intervention compared to a no-contact control group," said Ede. The researchers used the Personal Value Scale (PVS) and the Attitudes and Belief Scale-Abbreviated Version (ABS-AV) to measure changes in personal values and irrational beliefs before and after the intervention.

The results showed a significant reduction in NPVS among participants in the treatment group compared to the control group. "Our findings indicate that REBT was effective in reducing negative personal value systems," Ede noted. The study also found that REBT improved participants' self-worth and social acceptance. Future research could expand this approach to other physically challenged student populations, such as those who are deaf or mute. This study underscores the potential of REBT in addressing cognitive and emotional challenges among SLB, offering valuable insights for counseling psychologists and educators working with this vulnerable group.

Bibliography

1. Turner, M. J., & Barker, J. B. (2015). Examining the effects of rational emotive behavior therapy (REBT) on the irrational beliefs of blue-chip professionals. *Journal of Rational-Emotive & Cognitive-Behavior Therapy, 33*(1), 17–36. https://doi.org/10.1007/s10942-014-0200-9
2. Hyland, P., & Boduszek, D. (2012). A unitary or binary model of emotions: A discussion on a fundamental difference between cognitive therapy and rational emotive behavior therapy. *Journal of Humanistic and Social Sciences, 1*(1), 49–61.
3. Harrington, N. (2013). Irrational beliefs and socio-political extremism. *Journal of Rational-Emotive & Cognitive-Behavior Therapy, 31*, 167–178. https://doi.org/10.1007/s10942-013-0168-x
4. American Psychiatric Association. (2013) *Diagnostic and statistical manual of mental disorders (DSM-V)* (5th ed). American Psychiatric Association.
5. Russell, S. L., Haynos, A. F., Crow, S. J., & Fruzzetti, A. E. (2017). An experimental analysis of the affect regulation model of binge eating. *Appetite, 110*, 44–50. https://doi.org/10.1016/j.appet.2016.12.007
6. Woo, J. (2014). A survey of overweight, body shape perception and eating attitude of Korean female university students. *Journal of Exercise Nutrition & Biochemistry, 18*(3), 287–292. https://doi.org/10.5717/jenb.2014.18.3.287
7. Dorairaj, K., Thompson, K., Wilksch, S., Wade, T., Paxton, S., Austin, S., & Byrne, S. (2013). Risk factors for eating disorders: Investigating the relationships between global self-esteem, body-specific self-esteem and dietary restraint. *Journal of Eating Disorders, 1*(S1), O31. https://doi.org/10.1186/2050-2974-1-S1-O31
8. Ellis, A. (1994). *Reason and emotion in psychotherapy* (Rev ed). Carol Publishing Group.
9. Vernon, A. (1998). *The PASSPORT program: A journey through emotional, social, cognitive, and self-development, grades 9–12*. Research Press.
10. Ellis, A. (1995). Changing rational-emotive therapy (RET) to rational emotive behavior therapy (REBT). *Journal of Rational-Emotive and Cognitive-Behavior Therapy, 13*, 85–89.
11. Goodman, R., Meltzer, H., & Bailey, V. (1998). The strengths and difficulties questionnaire: A pilot study on the validity of the self-report version. *European Child & Adolescent Psychiatry, 7*, 125–130. https://doi.org/10.1007/s007870050057
12. Trip, S., Vernon, A., & McMahon, J. (2007). Effectiveness of rational-emotive education: A meta-analytical study. *Journal of Cognitive and Behavioral Psychotherapies, 7*, 81–93.
13. David, D. O., DiGiuseppe, R., Dobrean, A., Păsărelu, C. R., & Balazsi, R. (2019). The measurement of irrationality and rationality. In M. E. Bernard & W. Dryden (Eds.), *Advances in REBT: Theory, practice, research, measurement prevention and promotion* (pp. 79–100). Springer Nature.

14. Hyland, P., Shevlin, M., Adamson, G., & Boduszek, D. (2014). Modeling the structure of the attitudes and belief scale 2 using CFA and bifactor approaches: Toward the development of an abbreviated version. *Cognitive Behaviour Therapy, 43*(1), 60–71.
15. DiGiuseppe, R., Gorman, B., & Raptis, J. (2020). The factor structure of the attitudes and beliefs scale 2: Implications for rational emotive behavior therapy. *Journal of Rational Emotive and Cognitive Behavior Therapies, 38*(2), 111–142. https://doi.org/10.1007/s10942-020-00349-0
16. DiGiuseppe, R., Leaf, R., Gorman, B., & Robin, R. (2018). The development of a measure of irrational/ rational beliefs. *Journal of Rational-Emotive and Cognitive-Behavior Therapies, 36*(1), 47–79.
17. Agiurgioaei-Boie, A., Agiurgioaei, F., & DiGiuseppe, R. A. (Participant) (2011, August). *Cross cultural comparison of three cognitive-behavioral models for predicting emotional distress*. Poster Presentation at the 119th Annual APA Convention.
18. Dryden, W. (2002). *Idiosyncratic rational emotive behaviour therapy*. PCCS Books.
19. Fulton, J. J., Marcus, D. K., & Merkey, T. (2011). Irrational health beliefs and health anxiety. *Journal of Clinical Psychology, 67*, 527–538.
20. Kyrou, I., Kollia, N., Panagiotakos, D., et al. (2017). Association of depression and anxiety status with 10-year cardiovascular disease incidence among apparently healthy Greek adults: The ATTICA study. *European Journal of Preventive Cardiology, 24*, 145–152.
21. Papageorgiou, C., Panagiotakos, D. B., Pitsavos, C., et al. (2006). Association between plasma inflammatory markers and irrational beliefs; the ATTICA epidemiological study. *Progress in Neuropsychopharmacology & Biological Psychiatry, 30*, 1496–1503.
22. Querstret, D., & Cropley, M. (2013). Assessing treatments used to reduce rumination and/ or worry: A systematic review. *Clinical Psychology Review, 33*, 996–1009.
23. Vîslă, A., Flückiger, C., Grosse Holtforth, M., & David, D. (2016). Irrational beliefs and psychological distress: A meta-analysis. *Psychotherapy and Psychosomatics, 85*, 8–15.
24. Manios, Y., Panagiotakos, D. B., Pitsavos, C., Polychronopoulos, E., & Stefanadis, C. (2005). Implication of socio-economic status on the prevalence of overweight and obesity in Greek adults: The ATTICA study. *Health Policy, 74*, 224–232.
25. Gidron, Y., Davidson, K., & Bata, I. (1999). The short-term effects of a hostility-reduction intervention on male coronary heart disease patients. *Health Psychology, 18*, 416.
26. Freedland, K. E., Carney, R. M., Rich, M. W., Steinmeyer, B. C., & Rubin, E. H. (2015). Cognitive behavior therapy for depression and self-care in heart failure patients: A randomized clinical trial. *JAMA Internal Medicine, 175*, 1773–1782.
27. McLaughlin, T. J., Aupont, O., & Bambauer, K. Z. (2005). Improving psychologic adjustment to chronic illness in cardiac patients. *Journal of General Internal Medicine, 20*, 1084–1090.
28. Adegun, A. O., & Aremu, O. (2013). Effectiveness of career development and cognitive reframe therapy on irrational career thoughts among secondary school students in Ogun State, Nigeria. *The African Symposium, 13*(2), 94–103.
29. Ogbuanya, T. C., Eseadi, C., Orji, C. T., Anyanwu, J. I., Ede, M. O., & Bakare, J. (2017). Effect of rational-emotive behavior therapy on negative career thoughts of students in technical colleges in Nigeria. *Psychological Reports*. https://doi.org/10.1177/0033294117724449
30. Arulmani, G., Van Laar, D., & Easton, S. (2003). The influence of career beliefs and socio-economic status on the career decision making of high school students in India. *International Journal for Educational and Vocational Guidance, 3*(3), 204–220. https://doi.org/10.1023/B:IJVO.0000006599.92116.0a
31. Dipeolu, A., Reardon, R. C., Sampson, J. P., & Burkhead, J. (2002). The relationship between dysfunctional career thoughts and adjustment to disability in college students with learning disabilities. *Journal of Career Assessment, 10*(4), 413–427.

32. Jamali, Y., Araqi, V., & Kalantarkousheh, S. M. (2015). Function of dysfunctional career thoughts, procrastination and career indecision among Allameh Tabatab'i University students. *European Online Journal of Natural and Social Sciences*, *4*(1), 57–65.
33. Kleiman, T., Gati, I., Peterson, G. W., Sampson, J. P., Reardon, R. C., & Lenz, J. G. (2004). Dysfunctional thinking and difficulties in career decision making. *Journal of Career Assessment*, *12*(3), 312–331. https://doi.org/10.1177/1069072704266673
34. Osborn, D. S. (1998). The relationships among perfectionism, dysfunctional career thoughts and career indecision (Doctoral dissertation, Florida State University). *Dissertation Abstracts International*, *59*(10–A), 3746.
35. Peng, H., & Herr, E. L. (2002). Relation of career beliefs to career indecision among distance education adult college students in Taiwan. *Psychological Reports*, *90*, 803–813.
36. Savoly, K. D. D., & Owen, K. F. (2015). Irrational career beliefs among university applicants [Üniversite adaylarında meslek seçimine ilişkin akılcı olmayaninançlar]. *International Journal of Human Sciences*, *12*(2), 820–836. https://doi.org/10.14687/ijhs.v12i2.3357
37. Stead, G. B., Watson, M. B., & Foxcroft, C. D. (1993). The relation between career indecision and irrational beliefs among university students. *Journal of Vocational Behavior*, *42*(2), 155–169. https://doi.org/10.1006/jvbe.1993.1011
38. Turner, S. L., Ziebell, J., & Conkel, J. (2011). The career beliefs of inner-city adolescents. *Professional School Counseling*, *15*(1), 1–14.
39. Richman, D. R. (1993). Cognitive career counseling: A rational-emotive approach to career development. *Journal of Rational-Emotive & Cognitive-Behavior Therapy*, *11*(2), 91–98. https://doi.org/10.1007/BF01061234
40. Mahfar, M., Aslan, A. S., Noah, S. M., Ahmad, A., & Jaafar, W. M. (2014). Effects of rational emotive education module on irrational beliefs and stress among fully residential school students in Malaysia. *Procedia-Social and Behavioral Sciences*, *114*, 239–243. https://doi.org/10.1016/j.sbspro.2013.12.692
41. Vaida, S., Kállay, É., & Opre, A. (2008). Counseling in schools: A rational emotive behavior therapy (REBT) based intervention—A pilot study. *Cognition, Brain, Behavior*, *12*(1), 57–69.
42. Saunders, D., Peterson, G., Sampson, J., & Reardon, R. (2000). Relation of depression and dysfunctional career thinking to career indecision. *Journal of Vocational Behavior*, *56*(2), 288–298. https://doi.org/10.1006/jvbe.1999.1715
43. Sidiropoulou-Dimakakou, D., Argyropoulou, K., Drosos, N., & Terzaki, M. (2012). Career beliefs of Greek and non-Greek vocational education students. *Creative Education*, *3*(7), 1241–1250. https://doi.org/10.4236/ce.2012.37183
44. Ugwoke, S. C., Eseadi, C., Igbokwe, C. C., Chiaha, G. T., Nwaubani, O. O., Orji, C. T., et al. (2017). Effects of a rational-emotive health education intervention on stress management and irrational beliefs among technical college teachers in southeast Nigeria. *Medicine*, *96*(31), e7658. https://doi.org/10.1097/MD.0000000000007658
45. Jones, R. G. (1968). A measure of Ellis "irrational belief system'', with personality and maladjustment correlates. *Dissertation Abstracts International*, *29*, 4379.B–4380 B. (university microfilms. NO 696443).
46. Bora, C., Bernard, M. E., & Decsei-Radu, A. (2008). Teacher irrational belief scale—Preliminary norms for Romanian population. *Romanian Journal of Cognitive and Behavioral Psychotherapies*, *8*, 35–49.
47. Bermejo-Toro, L., & Prieto-Ursúa, M. (2006). Teachers' irrational beliefs and their relationship to distress in the profession. *Psychology in Spain*, *10*, 88–96.
48. Ellis, A., & Bernard, M. E. (Eds.). (1985) *Clinical applications of rational-emotive therapy*. Plenum Press.
49. Smith, T. W. (1989). Assessment in rational-emotive therapy: Empirical access to the ABCD model. In M. E. Bernard & R. DiGiuseppe (Eds.), *Inside rational-emotive therapy: A critical analysis of the theory and practice of Albert Ellis*. Academic Press.

50. Klassen, R. M., & Chiu, M. M. (2010). Effects on teachers' self-efficacy and job satisfaction: Teacher gender, years of experience, and job stress. *Journal of Educational Psychology*, *102*, 741–756. https://doi.org/10.1037/a0019237
51. Kalyva, E. (2013). Stress in Greek primary school teachers working under conditions of financial crisis. *Europe's Journal of Psychology*, *9*, 104–112. https://doi.org/10.5964/ejop.v9i1.488
52. McCarthy, C. J., Lambert, R. G., O'Donnell, M., & Melendres, L. T. (2009). The relation of elementary teachers' experience, stress, and coping resources to burnout symptoms. *Elementary School Journal*, *109*, 282–300. https://doi.org/10.1086/592308
53. Friedman, I. A. (2003). Self-efficacy and burnout in teaching: The importance of interpersonal-relations efficacy. *Social Psychology of Education*, *6*, 191–215.
54. Fisher, M. H. (2011). Factors influencing stress, burnout, and retention of secondary teachers. *Current Issues in Education*, *14*, 1–36.
55. Kyriacou, C. (2001). Teacher stress: Directions for future research. *Educational Review*, *53*, 27–35. https://doi.org/10.1080/00131910120033628
56. Popov, S., & Popov, S. (2015). The role of stressors at work and irrational beliefs in the prediction of teacher stress. *Primenjena Psihologija*, *8*, 5–23.
57. Khaledian, M., Babaee, H., & Amani, M. (2016). The relationship of psychological hardiness with irrational beliefs, emotional intelligence and work holism. *World Scientific News*, *26*, 86–100.
58. DiGiuseppe, R., & Bernard, M. E. (1990). The application of rational-emotive theory and therapy to school-aged children. *School Psychology Review*, *19*(3), 268.
59. Bernard, M. E., Ellis, A. E., & Terjesen, M. (2006). Rational-emotive behavioral approaches to childhood disorders: History, theory, practice, and research. In A. E. Ellis & M. E. Bernard (Eds.), *Rational emotive behavioral approaches to childhood disorders: Theory, practice, and research* (pp. 3–84). Springer.
60. Bernard, M., & Laws, W. (1988). *Childhood irrationality and mental health: Development of a scale*. Unpublished manuscript.
61. Smidt, D. L., Kassay, K., Terjesen, M., & White, C. (2009). *Irrational beliefs in predicting child behavior and emotions*. Poster presented at the annual American Psychological Association Conference.
62. Terjesen, M. D., Salhany, J., & Scuitto, M. J. (2009). A psychometric review of measures of irrational beliefs: Implications for psychotherapy. *Journal of Rational-Emotive & Cognitive Behavior Therapy*, *27*(2), 83–92.
63. Ellis, A. (1994). *Reason and emotional in psychotherapy: A comprehensive method of treating human disturbance. Revised and updated.* Birch Lane Press.
64. Ellis, A. (1962). *Reason and emotion in psychotherapy*. Lyle Stuart.
65. Ellis, A. (1976). The biological basis of human irrationality. *Journal of Individual Psychology*, *32*(2), 145–168.
66. Alberti, R. E., & Ellis, A. (2014). The biological basis of human irrationality. In J. Carlson, W. Knaus, J. Carlson, & W. Knaus (Eds.), *Albert Ellis revisited* (pp. 103–123). Routledge/Taylor & Francis Group.
67. Burgess, P. (1986). *Belief systems and emotional disturbance: Evaluation of the rational emotive model*. Unpublished doctoral dissertation. University of Melbourne.
68. Burgess, P. M. (1990). Toward resolution of conceptual issues in the assessment of belief systems in rational-emotive therapy. *Journal of Cognitive Psychotherapy*, *4*(2), 171–184.
69. Opris, D., & Macavei, B. (2007). The profile of emotional distress; norms for the Romanian population. *Journal of Cognitive and Behavioral Psychotherapies*, *7*(2), 139–158.
70. Beck, A. T., Ward, C. H., Mendelson, M., Mock, J., & Erbaugh, J. (1961). An inventory for measuring depression. *Archives Of General Psychiatry*, *4*, 561–571.

71. Agiurgioaei-Boie, A., Agiurgioaei-Boie, F., & DiGiuseppe, R. A. (Participant) (2011). *Cross cultural comparison of three cognitive-behavioral models for predicting emotional distress*. In Poster Presentation at the 119th Annual APA Convention.
72. Dupuy, H. J. (1984). The psychological general well-being (PGWB) index. In N. K. Wenger, M. E. Mattson, C. D. Furberg, & J. Elinson (Eds.), *Assessment of quality of life in clinical trials of cardiovascular therapies* (pp. 170–183). Lejacq Publishing Company.
73. Goldberg, D. P. (1972). *The detection of psychiatric illness by questionnaire: A technique for the identification and assessment of non-psychotic psychiatric illness*. Oxford University Press.
74. Diener, E., Emmons, R. A., Larsen, R. J., & Griffin, S. (1985). The satisfaction with life scale. *Journal of Personality Assessment*, *49*(1), 71–75. https://doi.org/10.1207/s15327752jpa4901_13
75. Spielberger, C. D., Gorsuch, R. L., & Lushene, R. (1970). *State—trait anxiety inventory*. Mind Garden Originally published by Consulting Psychologist Press.
76. Spielberger, C. D. (1979). *State—trait anger expression inventory* (Rev research ed). Mind Garden Originally published by Consulting Psychologist Press.
77. American Psychiatric Association. (1987). *Diagnostic and statistical manual of mental disorders*. (3rd rev ed). American Psychiatric Association.
78. Millon, T. (1987). *Manual for the MCMI-II* (2nd ed). National Computer Systems.
79. Leaf, R. C., DiGiuseppe, R., Ellis, A., & Mass, R. (1990). 'Healthy correlates of MCMI scales 4, 5, 6, and 7. *Journal of Personality Disorders*, *4*(3), 312–328. https://doi.org/10.1521/pedi.1990.4.3.312
80. Hayes, S., Strosahl, K., & Wilson, K. (2012). *Acceptance and commitment therapy* (2nd ed). Guilford Press.
81. David, D., & Szentagotai, A. (2006). Cognitions in cognitive-behavioral psychotherapies; toward an integrative model. *Clinical Psychology Review*, *26*, 284–298. https://doi.org/10.1016/j.cpr.2005.09.003
82. Hagger, M., & Orbell, S. (2003). A meta-analytic review of the common sense model of illness representations. *Psychology and Health*, *18*(2), 141–184.
83. Engel, J. M., Wilson, S., Tran, S. T., Jensen, M. P., & Ciol, M. A. (2013). Pain catastrophizing in youths with physical disabilities and chronic pain. *Journal of Pediatric Psychology*, *38*(2), 192–201.
84. Kelsey, R., Soderlund, K., & Arthur, C. (2004). Cardiovascular reactivity and adaptation to recurrent psychological stress: Replication and extension. *Psychophysiology*, *41*(6), 924–934.
85. Rosengren, A., Hawken, S., Ounpuu, S., Silwa, K., Zubaid, M., Almahmeed, W. A., et al. (2004). Association of psychosocial risk factors with risk of acute myocardial infarction in 11,119 cases and 13,648 controls from 52 countries (the INTERHEART study); case control study. *The Lancet*, *364*, 953–962.
86. Buenaver, L. F., Quartana, P. J., Grace, E. G., Sarlani, E., Simango, M., Edwards, R. R., et al. (2012). Evidence for indirect effects of pain catastrophizing on clinical pain among myofascial temporomandibular disorder participants: The mediating role of sleep disturbance. *Pain*, *153*(6), 1159–1166.
87. Plante, T. G., & Ford, M. B. (2000). The association between cardiovascular stress responsivity and perceived stress among subjects with irritable bowel syndrome and temporomandibular joint disorder: A preliminary analysis. *International Journal of Stress Management*, *2*, 103–119.
88. Cohen, S., Tyrrell, D. A. J., & Smith, A. P. (1991). Psychological stress and susceptibility to the common cold. *New England Journal of Medicine*, *325*, 606–612.
89. Martel, M. O., Wasan, A. D., Jamison, R. N., & Edwards, R. R. (2013). Catastrophic thinking and increased risk for prescription opioid misuse in patients with chronic pain. *Drug and Alcohol Dependence*, *132*(1–2), 335–341.

90. Ellis, A. (1971). Emotional disturbance and its treatment in a nutshell. *Canadian Counselor, 5*, 168–171.
91. Ellis, A. (1973). *Humanistic psychology: The rational-emotive approach*. Julian.
92. Arnow, B., Blasey, C., Constantino, M., Robinson, R., Hunkeler, E., Lee, J., et al. (2011). Catastrophizing, depression and pain-related disability. *General Hospital Psychiatry, 33*(2), 150–156.
93. Nieto, R., Raichle, K. A., Jensen, M. P., & Miró, J. (2012). Changes in pain-related beliefs, coping, and catastrophizing predict changes in pain intensity, pain interference, and psychological functioning in individuals with myotonic muscular dystrophy and facioscapulohumeral dystrophy. *The Clinical Journal of Pain, 28*(1), 47–54.
94. Sharpe, L. L., & Johnson, A. A. (2012). Pain related catastrophizing: We know it is important but why and how can we change it? *European Journal of Pain, 16*(7), 951–952.
95. Schrooten, M. S., Karsdorp, P. A., & Vlaeyen, J. S. (2013). Pain catastrophizing moderates the effects of pain contingent task interruptions. *European Journal of Pain, 17*(7), 1082–1092.
96. Twisk, J., Snel, J., Kemper, H., & Van-Mechelen, W. (1999). Changes in daily hassles and life events and the relation with coronary heart disease risk factors. A two-year longitudinal study in 27–29 year old males and females. *Journal of Psychosomatic Research, 46*, 229–240.
97. Wideman, T. H., Asmundson, G. J., Smeets, R. M., Zautra, A. J., Simmonds, M. J., Sullivan, M. L., et al. (2013). Rethinking the fear avoidance model: Toward a multidimensional framework of pain-related disability. *Pain, 154*(11), 2262–2265.
98. Boothby, J. L., Thorn, B. E., Overduin, L. Y., & Ward, L. C. (2004). Catastrophizing and perceived partner responses to pain. *Pain, 109*, 500–506.
99. Kraljevic, S., Banozic, A., Maric, A., Cosic, A., Sapunar, D., & Puljak, L. (2012). Parent pain catastrophizing is related to pain catastrophizing of their adult children. *International Journal of Behavioral Medicine, 19*(1), 115–119.
100. Welkom, J. S., Hwang, W., & Guite, J. W. (2013). Adolescent pain catastrophizing mediates the relationship between protective parental responses to pain and disability over time. *Journal of Pediatric Psychology, 38*(5), 541–550.
101. Cioffi, D., & Holloway, J. (1993). Delayed costs of suppressed pain. *Journal of Personality and Social Psychology, 64*(2), 272–282.
102. McCracken, L., & Eccleston, C. (2003). Coping or acceptance: What to do about chronic pain? *Pain, 105*, 197–204.
103. Turner, J., Jensen, M., & Romano, J. (2000). Do beliefs, coping, and catastrophizing independently predict functioning in patients with chronic pain? *Pain, 85*, 115–125.
104. de Vries, H. J., Reneman, M. F., Groothoff, J. W., Geertzen, J. B., & Brouwer, S. (2012). Factors promoting staying at work in people with chronic nonspecific musculoskeletal pain: A systematic review. *Disability and Rehabilitation: An International, Multidisciplinary Journal, 34*(6), 443–458.
105. Büyüköztürk, Ş. (2009). *Manual of data analysis for social sciences*. Pegem Academy.
106. Bryman, A., & Cramer, D. (2001). *Quantitative data analysis with SPSS Release 10 for Windows: A guide for social scientists*. Routledge.
107. Field, A. (2005). *Discovering statistics using SPSS*. SAGE.
108. Jones, R. G. (1969). A factored measure of Ellis's irrational belief system with personality and maladjustment correlates. (Doctoral Dissertation, Texas Technological College, 1968). *Dissertation Abstracts International, 69*, 6443.
109. Yurtal-Dinç, F. (1999). *Üniversite öğrencilerinin akılcı olmayan inançlarının bazı değişkenlere göre incelenmesi*. Yayınlanmamış Doktora Tezi, Gazi Üniversitesi Eğitim Bilimleri Enstitüs.
110. DiGiuseppe, R., Gorman, B., & Raptis, J. (2020). *The factor structure of the Attitudes and Beliefs Scale-2* (Manuscript submitted).

111. Ejekwu, L. B. (2017). Influence of parental influence on students' social well-being. *Journal of Emotional Development*, *1*(1), 23–35.
112. Theodorson, G. A., & Achilles, G. T.(1969). *Modern dictionary of sociology* (pp. 456–457) Thomas Y. Crowell Company.
113. Pant, P., & Joshi, P. K. (2016). A comparative study of emotional stability of visually impaired students studying at secondary level in inclusive setup and special schools. *Journal of Education and Practice*, *7*(22), 53–58.
114. Hughes, M. E. (1995). *The changing perceptions and attitudes towards children with a vision impairment in high schools. A professional study submitted to the school of education being part requirement for the degree of Master of Education Course*. Faculty of Education, University of Tasmania-Hobart.
115. Okechukwu, U. (2019). Value system and visual impaired value impasse. *Journal of Special Education in Developing Areas*, *1*(2), 20–29.
116. Ojumu, B. (2016). *Civic education {JSS2}: Values*. Technology Transforming Education.
117. Uzomba, L. K. (2011). Depressant value system and educational goals and objectives actualization. *Journal of Physically Challenged in Developing Areas*, *1*(2), 31–44.
118. Yusuf, M. A. (2001). *Principles and practices of behavior modifications*. Thomsons Printing Press.
119. Aldahadha, B. (2018). Disputing irrational beliefs among convicted terrorists and extremist beliefs. *Journal of Rational-Emotive & Cognitive-Behavior Therapy*. https://doi.org/10.1007/s10942-018-0293-7
120. Yang, J., & Han, K. S. (2020). A rational emotive behavior therapy-based intervention for binge eating behavior management among female students: A quasi-experimental study. *Journal of Eating Disorders*. https://doi.org/10.1186/s40337-020-00347-8
121. David, O. A., Cardoş, R. A. I., & Matu, S. (2018). Changes in irrational beliefs are responsible for the efficacy of the REThink therapeutic game in preventing emotional disorders in children and adolescents: Mechanisms of change analysis of a randomized clinical trial. *European Child & Adolescent Psychiatry*. https://doi.org/10.1007/s00787-018-1195-z
122. DiGiuseppe, R., Gorman, B., Raptis, J., Agiurgioaei-Boie, A., Agiurgioaei, F., Leaf, R., & Robin, M. W. (2021). The development of a short form of an irrational/rational beliefs scale. *Journal of Rational-Emotive & Cognitive-Behavior Therapy*. https://doi.org/10.1007/s10942-021-00386-3
123. Vassou, C., Georgousopoulou, E. N., Yannakoulia, M., Chrysohoou, C., Papageorgiou, C., Pitsavos, C., Cropley, M., & Panagiotakos, D. B. (2022). Exploring the role of irrational beliefs, lifestyle behaviors, and educational status in 10-year cardiovascular disease risk: The ATTICA epidemiological study. *International Journal of Behavioral Medicine*. https://doi.org/10.1007/s12529-022-10091-9
124. Ogbuanya, T. C., Eseadi, C., Orji, C. T., Anyanwu, J. I., Joachim, O. C., & Otu, M. S. (2017). The effect of rational emotive behavior therapy on irrational career beliefs of students of electrical electronics and other engineering trades in technical colleges in Nigeria. *Journal of Rational-Emotive & Cognitive-Behavior Therapy*. https://doi.org/10.1007/s10942-017-0282-2
125. Bernard, M. E. (2016). Teacher beliefs and stress. *Journal of Rational-Emotive & Cognitive-Behavior Therapy*. https://doi.org/10.1007/s10942-016-0238-y
126. Terjesen, M. D., Kassay, K. S., & Anderson, D. L. (2017). Evaluation of the psychometric properties of a measure of child irrationality. *Journal of Rational-Emotive & Cognitive-Behavior Therapy*. https://doi.org/10.1007/s10942-017-0269-z
127. DiGiuseppe, R., Leaf, R., Gorman, B., & Robin, M. W. (2017). The development of a measure of irrational/rational beliefs. *Journal of Rational-Emotive & Cognitive-Behavior Therapy*. https://doi.org/10.1007/s10942-017-0273-3

128. Smith, K., Herman, M., & Smith, C. (2015). The role of catastrophizing beliefs in effective chronic pain treatment. *Journal of Rational-Emotive & Cognitive-Behavior Therapy*. https://doi.org/10.1007/s10942-015-0220-0
129. Artiran, M., & DiGiuseppe, R. (2020). A Turkish translation of a measure of irrational and rational beliefs: Reliability, validity studies and confirmation of the four cognitive processes model. *Journal of Rational-Emotive & Cognitive-Behavior Therapy*. https://doi.org/10.1007/s10942-020-00340-9
130. Ede, M. O., Okeke, C. I., & Chukwu, C. L. (2021). Assessing the efficacy of rational emotive behavior intervention for visually impaired upper basic school children with negative self-belief/personal value system. *Journal of Rational-Emotive & Cognitive-Behavior Therapy*. https://doi.org/10.1007/s10942-021-00419-x

Chapter 3
Techniques and Effectiveness of REBT

Introduction by the Editor

Rational Emotive Behavioral Therapy (REBT), founded by Albert Ellis in the mid-twentieth century, is one of the most influential approaches in cognitive-behavioral therapy (CBT). Rooted in the idea that irrational beliefs cause emotional and behavioral disturbances, REBT teaches individuals to recognize and replace these unhelpful beliefs with more rational and adaptive ones. This chapter delves into the core techniques of REBT and assesses its effectiveness across a range of settings and populations, with a particular focus on research studies that showcase its application in diverse contexts. The chapter brings together a variety of research papers, providing the reader with insights into how REBT techniques have been employed to address different psychological, emotional, and behavioral challenges. The primary aim of this chapter is to provide a comprehensive overview of REBT's techniques, applications, and effectiveness. We will discuss how REBT is used to help individuals manage and overcome emotional difficulties, improve mental health outcomes, and enhance coping skills across various life situations. The research papers included in this chapter represent a wide array of settings, from educational interventions targeting students to clinical studies on mental health conditions like depression, anxiety, and addiction. Furthermore, the papers also explore the application of REBT in non-clinical contexts, such as improving workplace environments and family dynamics, illustrating the therapy's broad reach.

The research papers included in this chapter were carefully selected based on their relevance to understanding REBT's techniques and outcomes. Each study explores a different aspect of REBT, from its comparison with other therapeutic modalities, such as client-centered therapy, to its effectiveness in specific cultural or geographical contexts. These papers not only provide insights into how REBT works but also highlight the challenges and limitations of applying REBT in real-world settings. By including studies that examine REBT's efficacy with different

M. Siddique et al., *Rational Emotive Behavior Therapy*,
https://doi.org/10.1007/978-3-032-32191-6_3

age groups, cultures, and mental health issues, this chapter aims to give readers a well-rounded understanding of the therapy's utility and its broader implications.

Through the synthesis of these research papers, readers will learn how REBT is applied to various psychological disorders, such as anger, anxiety, depression, and addiction, as well as how it is used to promote emotional well-being in everyday life. The reader will also gain insight into the underlying techniques of REBT, such as cognitive restructuring, the ABCDE model (Activating event, Beliefs, Consequences, Disputation, and New Effect), and behavioral interventions. Additionally, the chapter highlights the successes and limitations of these techniques, offering an evaluation of the effectiveness of REBT in different contexts.

Inclusion of these particular studies allows for an exploration of the breadth of REBT's applicability. Some studies focus on the clinical setting, where REBT is used as a primary therapeutic approach for individuals with mental health disorders such as depression, internet addiction, and anger issues. For instance, the study "Rational Emotive Behavior Therapy Compared to Client-Centered Therapy for Outpatients" (Artiran & DiGiuseppe, 2021) directly compares the effectiveness of REBT with another well-known therapeutic approach, providing evidence of REBT's superior efficacy in treating outpatient mental health conditions. Another significant paper, "Rational Emotive Behavior Therapy for Dysfunctional Anger: A Case Study"(Kabadayi & Yuksel, 2021), presents a practical case study highlighting how REBT can be successfully employed to help individuals manage dysfunctional anger, a common emotional issue.

In addition to these clinical applications, several studies in this chapter examine REBT in educational and community-based settings. For example, the study "Reducing Negative Value System in Students: The Impacts of Rational Emotive Behavioral Education" (Abiogu et al., 2021) explores how REBT can be used to reshape students' value systems and improve their emotional regulation. In this case, REBT not only addresses personal emotional distress but also aims to cultivate a more rational and healthy value system in young people, potentially preventing long-term psychological issues. Another study, "Rational Emotive Digital Storytelling Therapy for Improving HIV/AIDS Knowledge and Risk Perception Among Schoolchildren" (Ezegbe et al., 2019), demonstrates how REBT can be integrated with digital tools like storytelling to improve health knowledge and attitudes among schoolchildren, showing the flexibility of REBT to adapt to contemporary digital learning environments.

Moreover, the chapter includes studies that highlight the efficacy of REBT in addressing childhood trauma and stress, as seen in the paper "Effects of Cognitive Restructuring Intervention Program of Rational-Emotive Behavior Therapy on Adverse Childhood Stress in Nigeria" (Eseadi et al., 2015). This study underscores the potential of REBT in mitigating the psychological effects of childhood trauma, suggesting that early interventions can promote resilience and emotional regulation in children who have experienced stress. Such findings are crucial, as they emphasize REBT's capacity to serve as both a preventive and remedial tool for emotional disturbances stemming from adverse early-life experiences.

REBT's application in the workplace and in occupational settings is another area explored in this chapter. The study "Effects of Rational Emotive Behavior Occupational Intervention on Perceptions of Work Value and Ethical Practices" (Abiogu et al., 2021) demonstrates how REBT can improve individuals' perceptions of work values and ethical practices, providing evidence that REBT is not limited to traditional therapeutic environments but can be employed to enhance the ethical and emotional dimensions of workplace behavior. These findings are significant because they suggest that REBT can contribute to improving organizational culture and promoting healthier interpersonal dynamics in professional settings.

One of the primary techniques of REBT is the ABCDE model, which helps individuals understand the connection between their thoughts, emotions, and behaviors. This model is frequently applied in various studies included in this chapter. For example, "Effect of Rational Emotive Behavior Therapy Program on Depressive Symptoms Among University Students with Blindness in Nigeria" (Onuigbo et al., 2018) highlights how REBT helps students with blindness cope with depressive symptoms by challenging irrational beliefs and encouraging healthier cognitive patterns. This model has been applied successfully across multiple studies, demonstrating that REBT is a versatile approach that can be customized to suit individual needs, regardless of the person's condition or background. The chapter also highlights some of the challenges and limitations of using REBT in certain contexts. Although REBT has demonstrated effectiveness in treating a range of psychological issues, there are concerns about the accessibility and consistency of its application. Studies indicate that proper training for therapists and professionals is crucial to ensure that the therapeutic interventions are implemented correctly. For example, the study "Testing the Efficacy of Family Health-Model of REBT on Family Values and Quality of Family Life Among Parents of Children with Visual Impairment" (Ede et al., 2021) emphasizes the importance of tailoring REBT interventions to specific family dynamics and cultural contexts. In this case, the research suggests that the integration of REBT into family therapy requires not only a solid understanding of the family's structure and values but also an understanding of how cultural factors may influence the effectiveness of the interventions.

Another limitation is the need for more longitudinal research to assess the long-term effectiveness of REBT. While numerous studies demonstrate the immediate benefits of REBT in treating conditions such as anger, anxiety, and depression, fewer studies focus on its long-term impact. For example, the "Warrior Resilience and Thriving" study (Jarrett, 2013) on military personnel suggests that REBT can play a role in preparing soldiers for post-traumatic growth and resilience. However, additional research is needed to determine how long-lasting these effects are and whether they persist over time without continued intervention. This is critical gap in the literature, as understanding the long-term outcomes of REBT could help refine therapeutic strategies and improve treatment protocols.

Furthermore, the adaptability of REBT to digital and online platforms is an emerging area of research that holds considerable promise. The study on digital storytelling therapy (Ezegbe et al., 2019) demonstrates that REBT can be effectively integrated into digital formats, such as online counseling, educational games, and interactive storytelling tools, offering a more accessible means of reaching individuals who might otherwise not have access to traditional face-to-face therapy. As digital mental health tools become increasingly common, further exploration into how REBT can be adapted for online platforms will be crucial for expanding its reach.

Despite these challenges, the research included in this chapter highlights several key findings that demonstrate the effectiveness of REBT in a variety of settings. One of the most significant findings is that REBT is highly effective in reducing emotional distress, including anger, depression, and anxiety. Numerous studies report positive outcomes from the application of REBT techniques, suggesting that individuals exposed to REBT experience reduced symptoms of these conditions. Furthermore, REBT fosters the development of rational thinking, which empowers individuals to approach problems in a more adaptive and constructive manner. This cognitive shift is often associated with improved mental health and enhanced life satisfaction.

Another major takeaway from the chapter is the recognition that REBT is not a one-size-fits-all therapeutic approach. The flexibility of REBT techniques allows them to be tailored to a wide range of conditions, populations, and cultural contexts. From young school children learning about HIV/AIDS risk to university students coping with blindness-induced depression, REBT proves its versatility in addressing diverse needs. However, this flexibility also necessitates careful consideration of how REBT is applied, taking into account the individual's unique circumstances and the context in which they are receiving therapy.

In conclusion, this chapter provides a detailed examination of the techniques and effectiveness of Rational Emotive Behavioral Therapy. The studies included in this chapter highlight REBT's success in treating a variety of psychological conditions, improving coping skills, and fostering positive behavioral change. Despite its many strengths, there are still significant gaps in the research, particularly regarding its long-term effectiveness and application in complex disorders.

Machine Generated Summaries

Disclaimer: The summaries in this chapter were generated from Springer Nature publications using extractive AI auto-summarization: An extraction-based summarizer aims to identify the most important sentences of a text using an algorithm and uses those original sentences to create the auto-summary (unlike generative AI). As the constituted sentences are machine selected, they may not fully reflect the body of the work, so we strongly advise that the original content is read and cited. The auto generated summaries were curated by the editor to meet Springer Nature publication standards. To cite this content, please refer to the original papers.

Machine generated keywords: value, nigeria, stress, child, anger, family, victim, disorder, affect, posttraumatic, client, report, adult, teacher, member

Reducing Negative Value System in Students: The Impacts of Rational Emotive Behavioural Education [111]

This is a machine-generated summary of:

Abiogu, Godwin C.; Ede, Moses Onyemaechi; Mezieobi, Daniel I.; Nwosu, Nneka; Ogheneakoke, Clifford E.; Ujah, Patrick; Chukwuemeka, Ezurike A.; Agbigwe, Ifeanyichukwu B.: Reducing Negative Value System in Students: The Impacts of Rational Emotive Behavioural Education [111]

Published in: Journal of Rational-Emotive & Cognitive-Behavior Therapy (2021)

Link to original: https://doi.org/10.1007/s10942-021-00387-2

If you want to cite the papers, please refer to the original.

For technical reasons we could not place the page where the original quote is coming from.

Research Highlights

Values are beliefs that are tied inextricably to emotion, motivational constructs, and transcend specific actions and situations. Despite efforts by the Federal Government of Nigeria to promote a positive value system, many Nigerian students still exhibit immoral conduct and negative values. Now, a new study by Godwin C. Abiogu and colleagues investigates the impact of Rational Emotive Behavioral Education (REBE) on promoting desirable value systems among secondary school students in Nigeria.

The study involved secondary school students from Enugu State, Nigeria, who were randomly assigned to either an intervention group or a no-contact control group. The intervention group participated in a three-month REBE program consisting of 12 sessions that covered topics such as the meaning of values, the relationship between beliefs, behaviors, emotions, and values, and techniques for disputing false values. The program was delivered by trained therapists using cognitive-behavioral techniques like cognitive disputation and restructuring. The Life Values Inventory (LVI) was used to measure the participants' value systems before and after the intervention.

The results showed that participants in the intervention group had significantly higher mean scores for desirable value systems compared to those in the control group at both posttest and follow-up stages. This indicates that REBE effectively reduced negative value systems by increasing positive value systems among Nigerian students. According to Abiogu, "The reduction in negative value systems gave rise to increased positive value systems," suggesting that cognitive-behavioral approaches can be extended beyond clinical settings to address social and cultural issues. Future research should explore integrating REBE into school curricula and teacher training programs to sustain these positive outcomes.

Rational Emotive Behavior Therapy Compared to Client-Centered Therapy for Outpatients: A Randomized Clinical Trial with a Three Months Follow up [112]

This is a machine-generated summary of:

Artiran, Murat; DiGiuseppe, Raymond: Rational Emotive Behavior Therapy Compared to Client-Centered Therapy for Outpatients: A Randomized Clinical Trial with a Three Months Follow up [112]

Published in: Journal of Rational-Emotive & Cognitive-Behavior Therapy (2021)

Link to original: https://doi.org/10.1007/s10942-021-00408-0

If you want to cite the papers, please refer to the original.

For technical reasons we could not place the page where the original quote is coming from.

Research Highlights

Cognitive behavior therapy (CBT) has long been a cornerstone in the treatment of various psychological disorders, with Rational Emotive Behavior Therapy (REBT) being one of its earliest forms. REBT uniquely posits that irrational beliefs are the primary cause of psychological disturbances and that altering these beliefs can lead to significant emotional and behavioral improvements. Despite strong evidence supporting REBT's efficacy, many earlier studies did not meet modern standards for empirically supported treatments. Now, a new study by Murat Artiran and colleagues aims to address this gap by comparing the effectiveness of REBT with Humanistic Client-Centered Therapy (HCCT) in treating Generalized Anxiety Disorder (GAD) with comorbid mild depression.

Artiran et al. conducted a randomized controlled trial involving 36 Participants from a counseling center in Istanbul, Turkey. Participants were randomly assigned to either the REBT or HCCT group and underwent 12 weeks of therapy. The REBT group received therapy from an experienced REBT supervisor using a structured manual, while the HCCT group was treated by three therapists trained in HCCT. The study employed various psychometric measures, including the Beck Depression Inventory and Beck Anxiety Inventory, to assess changes in irrational beliefs, depression, anxiety, life satisfaction, and both healthy and unhealthy negative emotions. Statistical analyses, including split-plot ANOVA and Reliable Change Index (RCI), were used to evaluate the outcomes.

The study found that while both therapies led to significant reductions in irrational beliefs and unhealthy negative emotions over time, REBT demonstrated more substantial improvements across multiple variables compared to HCCT. Specifically, REBT was more effective in reducing symptoms of depression and anxiety and enhancing ontological well-being aspects such as activation and regret. "Our findings suggest that REBT not only alleviates psychological distress but also supports positive psychological constructs," says Artiran. Future research should explore longer-term effects and include larger sample sizes to further validate these findings. This study underscores the need for continued research into the distinctive features of classical REBT to solidify its standing as an empirically supported treatment.

Rational Emotive Digital Storytelling Therapy for Improving HIV/AIDS Knowledge and Risk Perception Among Schoolchildren: A Group Randomized Trial [113]

This is a machine-generated summary of:

Ezegbe, Bernedeth N.; Eseadi, Chiedu; Ede, Moses Onyemaechi; Igbo, Janet N.; Aneke, Anthonia; Nnamani, Amuche; Ugwu, Gloria C.; Ugwoezuonu, Amada U.; Elizabeth, Ebizie; Ede, Kelechi R.; Chinweuba, Ngozi H.; Ede, Augustina O.: Rational Emotive Digital Storytelling Therapy for Improving HIV/AIDS Knowledge and Risk Perception Among Schoolchildren: A Group Randomized Trial [113]

Published in: Journal of Rational-Emotive & Cognitive-Behavior Therapy (2019)

Link to original: https://doi.org/10.1007/s10942-019-00316-4

If you want to cite the papers, please refer to the original.

For technical reasons we could not place the page where the original quote is coming from.

Research Highlights

Children affected by HIV/AIDS face numerous challenges, including lack of caregivers, limited access to education, and increased vulnerability to the disease.

Despite a significant decrease in new infections among children between 2000 and 2015, the number of children affected by HIV/AIDS remains high. Now a new study by Bernedeth N. Ezegbe and colleagues explores whether rational emotive digital storytelling (REDStory) can improve knowledge and risk perception of HIV/AIDS among Nigerian schoolchildren.

The study involved 80 schoolchildren from public and private secondary schools in Ebonyi State, Nigeria. Participants were divided into a treatment group that received the REDStory intervention and a waitlisted control group. The REDStory intervention integrated rational-emotive education with HIV/AIDS audio-visual resources from social media platforms like Facebook and YouTube. Children watched videos containing HIV/AIDS stories and information during group sessions and at home, followed by discussions led by therapists to explore their knowledge and perceived risks of HIV/AIDS. The researchers used self-report instruments to measure HIV knowledge and perceived risk before, immediately after, and three months post-intervention.

The results showed that the REDStory intervention significantly improved both the knowledge and perceived risk of HIV/AIDS among the schoolchildren in the treatment group compared to those in the control group. "Rational emotive digital storytelling therapy was therapeutically helpful in raising the level of HIV knowledge among schoolchildren who benefited from it," said Ezegbe. The study suggests that integrating REBT principles with digital storytelling can be an effective method for educating children about HIV/AIDS. Future research should consider larger sample sizes, include out-of-school children, and explore long-term impacts to further validate these findings.

Effects of Cognitive Restructuring Intervention Program of Rational-Emotive Behavior Therapy on Adverse Childhood Stress in Nigeria [114]

This is a machine-generated summary of:

Eseadi, Chiedu; Anyanwu, Joy I.; Ogbuabor, Shulamite E.; Ikechukwu-Ilomuanya, Amaka B.: Effects of Cognitive Restructuring Intervention Program of Rational-Emotive Behavior Therapy on Adverse Childhood Stress in Nigeria [114]

Published in: Journal of Rational-Emotive & Cognitive-Behavior Therapy (2015)

Link to original: https://doi.org/10.1007/s10942-015-0229-4

If you want to cite the papers, please refer to the original.

For technical reasons we could not place the page where the original quote is coming from.

Research Highlights

**Adverse effects of stress on quality of life of people of all ages had attracted the attention of researchers. Even children experience stress in a way that it could affect them later in life depending on the stressors. Adverse childhood stress refers to traumatic childhood experience in the form of child maltreatment, severe abuse and neglect, which impairs a child's ability and well-being during development, with damaging effects on learning, behavior, adjustment, and health across the lifespan. Adverse stress at childhood disrupts a person's normal state of well-being and is capable of affecting health and behavior later in life with psychophysiological consequences. Some instances of adverse childhood stress include child sexual abuse, physical abuse, and witnessing of intimate partner violence (Centers for Disease Control and Prevention; MiddleBrooks and Audage). Previous studies pointed out some psychological effects of stress like anxiety, depression, interpersonal problems, and ineffective cognitive processes. Other researchers also indicated that some of the negative physiological effects of stress include hypertension, high levels of muscle tension, and lowering of immune system defenses stated that stress results in symptoms such as rise in the blood pressure, release of hormones, quickness of breath, tightening of muscles, perspiration, and increased cardiac activity. However, Adegoke argued that mild stress may be desirable in stimulating or motivating individual towards laudable achievement whereas, on a more severe level, stress can be dangerous and damaging with physical, psychological, and behavioral harmful effects on its victims. The differences in experimental findings and alternative theoretical models highlight the complex nature of gender-specific stress response, which may be dependent on the type of stressor/challenge, experimental procedure, outcome measured, and subject status. According to Middlebrooks and Audage, childhood stress can lead to health problems later in life including alcoholism, depression, eating disorders, heart disease, cancer, and other chronic diseases. There also appears to be differences in stress experience and effects between men and women. For instance, a study by Matud revealed that women scored significantly higher than men in chronic stress and minor daily stressors; somatic symptoms; psychological distress; also rated women's life events as more negative and less controllable than men; listed family- and health-related events more frequently than men. Similarly Kajantie & Phillips found that women are at greater risk for depression & anxiety while men are at risk for different types of stress-related disorders.

Now a new study by Chiedu Eseadi et al., examines the effects cognitive restructuring intervention program (CRIP) within rational-emotive behavior therapy (REBT) could have on reduction of irrational behaviors/thoughts arising from adverse childhood stress among Nigerian subjects.

The researchers conducted their study with participants from Nsukka Town in Enugu State located in southeastern Nigeria. The participants were identified as victims of adverse childhood stress through self-report questionnaires. The study used repeated measures design which allowed the researchers to measure at time the participant's level of irrational thoughts/behaviors before & after intervention program (CRIP-REBT). Participants were randomly assigned to control group & treatment group. The treatment group received weeks full intervention & weeks follow-up meetings while control group received no intervention. The researchers applied repeated measures ANOVA to see improvement/change in individual participant & across control/treatment groups' behaviors after intervention program.

The study found significant main effect CRIP-REBT on irrational thoughts/behaviors arising from adverse childhood stress among treatment group compared to control group. Through this therapy irrational thoughts/behaviors arising from adverse childhood stress significantly reduced treatment group compared control group lowered significantly end intervention compared beginning treatment group measuring Time participants' level rational/irrational thoughts/behaviors associated adverse childhood stress researchers able determine how change turn led changes participants' levels stress findings support previous studies showed REBT effectively reduce stress findings further agree previous studies application cognitive restructuring remediating problem behaviors significant main effects present findings also confirmed Rector's assertion childhood experiences events while not focus cognitive behavior therapy may reviewed help people understand address emotional upset emerged early life learn how experiences.

The Effect of Rational Emotive Behaviour Therapy on Post-Traumatic Depression in Flood Victims [115]

This is a machine-generated summary of:

Ede, Moses Onyemaechi; Adene, Friday M.; Okeke, Chinedu Ifedi; Mezieobi, Daniel I.; Isiwu, Evelyn Nkiruka; Abdullahi, Yakubu: The Effect of Rational Emotive Behaviour Therapy on Post-Traumatic Depression in Flood Victims [115]

Published in: Journal of Rational-Emotive & Cognitive-Behavior Therapy (2021)

Link to original: https://doi.org/10.1007/s10942-021-00401-7

If you want to cite the papers, please refer to the original.

For technical reasons we could not place the page where the original quote is coming from.

Research Highlights

Flooding is one of the most disruptive and costly natural disasters worldwide, often resulting from prolonged rainfall, dam breaks, or inadequate drainage systems. In Nigeria, flooding has been exacerbated by climate change and poor urban planning, affecting millions and causing significant loss of life and property. Now a new study by Moses Onyemaechi Ede and colleagues investigates the impact of Rational Emotive Behavioral Therapy (REBT) on posttraumatic depression among flood victims in Kogi State, Nigeria.

The study employed a pretest-posttest control group design involving 60 Participants who met the criteria for inclusion based on their depression levels. Participants were randomly assigned to either an REBT treatment group or a waitlist control group. The REBT intervention consisted of 12 sessions over six weeks, focusing on identifying and disputing irrational beliefs that contribute to depressive symptoms. The Hamilton Depression Rating Scale (HDRS) and Goldberg's Depression Scale (GDS) were used to measure outcomes at pretest, posttest, and follow-up stages. According to Ede, "The REBT model was instrumental in helping participants reframe their thoughts and reduce depressive symptoms."

The findings revealed that REBT significantly reduced depressive symptoms among flood victims compared to the control group. At post-treatment and follow-up stages, participants in the REBT group showed marked improvement in their depression scores on both HDRS and GDS scales. This study underscores the efficacy of REBT in addressing posttraumatic depression among disaster victims. Ede suggests that "Future research should explore the application of REBT in other disaster contexts to build a comprehensive database for mental health interventions." The study highlights the need for mental health support systems for flood victims and suggests that REBT could be a valuable tool in mitigating the psychological impact of natural disasters.

Internet Addiction in Adolescents: A Rational Emotive and Cognitive Behavior Therapy Perspective [116]

This is a machine-generated summary of:

Stojković, Irena; Vukosavljević-Gvozden, Tatjana; David, Isidora; Purić, Danka: Internet Addiction in Adolescents: A Rational Emotive and Cognitive Behavior Therapy Perspective [116]

Published in: Journal of Rational-Emotive & Cognitive-Behavior Therapy (2022)

Link to original: https://doi.org/10.1007/s10942-022-00445-3

If you want to cite the papers, please refer to the original.

For technical reasons we could not place the page where the original quote is coming from.

Research Highlights

During the last decades, the Internet has become a widespread means of gaining information, communication, and developing social networks. The number of Internet users is increasing worldwide, with the majority being adolescents and young people. However, some individuals develop excessive Internet use, which negatively impacts their relationships, academic performance, and professional life. Now a new study by Irena Stojković and colleagues aims to test whether irrational beliefs are positively related to Internet addiction and if psychopathological tendencies mediate this relationship.

The study involved adolescents from a college preparatory high school in Belgrade, Serbia. Participants completed questionnaires assessing irrational and rational beliefs using the Serbian Version of the General Attitude and Belief Scale (SGABS), psychopathological symptoms using the Symptom Checklist-90-Revised (SCL-90-R), and Internet addiction using the Internet Addiction Test (IAT). The researchers performed a Principal Component Analysis on SGABS items to identify factors of irrational beliefs and used multiple mediation models to test the mediating effect of psychopathology on the relationship between irrational beliefs and Internet addiction. The results showed that irrational beliefs had a direct positive effect on Internet addiction and that obsessive-compulsive tendencies and phobic anxiety partially mediated this relationship.

The findings suggest that irrational beliefs contribute to Internet addiction both directly and indirectly through specific psychopathological tendencies. This supports cognitive-behavioral frameworks that emphasize maladaptive cognitions as central to developing Internet addiction. Stojković notes, "Our results have implications for prevention and treatment, suggesting that changing irrational beliefs may help individuals overcome maladaptive internet use." Future research should explore specific irrational beliefs related to internet use and investigate these relationships longitudinally to better understand causality.

Rational-Emotive Behavior Therapy for Dysfunctional Anger: A Case Study [117]

This is a machine-generated summary of:

Kabadayi, Fedai; Yuksel, Galip: Rational-Emotive Behavior Therapy for Dysfunctional Anger: A Case Study [117]

Published in: Journal of Rational-Emotive & Cognitive-Behavior Therapy (2021)

Link to original: https://doi.org/10.1007/s10942-020-00384-x

If you want to cite the papers, please refer to the original.

For technical reasons we could not place the page where the original quote is coming from.

Research Highlights

Anger is a complex emotion that can be both functional and dysfunctional, depending on the context and intensity. While functional anger can mobilize individuals to address threats or injustices, dysfunctional anger often leads to negative consequences for oneself and others. Despite its significance, anger is not categorized in the DSM, and there is limited research on its treatment compared to other emotions like depression and anxiety. Now, a new study by Fedai Kabadayi and colleagues aims to fill this gap by exploring the effectiveness of Rational Emotive Behavior Therapy (REBT) in treating dysfunctional anger in a non-clinical case involving a young Turkish woman.

The study utilized an A–B–A single-case design, involving baseline, intervention, and maintenance phases. The client, a university student experiencing intense anger towards her long-distance boyfriend, underwent eight REBT sessions followed by a three-week follow-up. The therapy focused on disputing irrational beliefs, cognitive restructuring, and imaginal exposure. "The client realized that her existing irrational thoughts should change," Kabadayi notes. Measurements were taken using the Oxford Happiness Questionnaire—Short Form and the Trait Anger and Anger Expression Scale to assess changes in happiness and anger levels. The sessions were recorded for supervision purposes, ensuring adherence to REBT principles.

The findings revealed significant improvements in the client's emotional regulation and relationship satisfaction. "Her thoughts toward her boyfriend were more flexible, and she was happier and less angry," Kabadayi reports. This study highlights the potential of REBT in addressing dysfunctional anger within collectivist cultures like Turkey, where interdependent self-construals may influence therapy outcomes. Future research should explore REBT's effectiveness in different cultural contexts and with various irrational beliefs. Additionally, incorporating mid-test measurements could provide more comprehensive insights into therapy progress. This case study serves as a valuable guide for mental health practitioners aiming to apply classic REBT techniques to treat dysfunctional anger effectively.

Effect of School-Based Rational-Emotive Behaviour Program on Burnout Among Adult Learners: Moderating Influence of Participants' Demographic Variables [118]

This is a machine-generated summary of:

Iremeka, Felicia Ukamaka; Eseadi, Chiedu; Ezenwaji, Chisom; Ezenwaji, Ifeyinwa O.; Okide, Charity Chinelo; Ogbonna, Chimaobi Samuel; Onwuchekwe, Stanley Ikenna: Effect of School-based Rational-Emotive Behaviour Program on Burnout Among Adult Learners: Moderating Influence of Participants' Demographic Variables [118]

Published in: Journal of Rational-Emotive & Cognitive-Behavior Therapy (2021)

Link to original: https://doi.org/10.1007/s10942-021-00393-4

If you want to cite the papers, please refer to the original.

For technical reasons we could not place the page where the original quote is coming from.

Research Highlights

Burnout among adult learners, particularly those who are also teachers, is a significant issue in Nigeria due to the multiple stressors they face from family, work, and academic responsibilities. Despite the prevalence of burnout, there is a lack of studies addressing its assessment and management among this group. Now a new study by Felicia Ukamaka Iremeka and colleagues at the University of Nigeria investigates the effectiveness of a school-based Rational Emotive Behaviour Therapy (REBT) program in reducing burnout among adult learners who are teachers.

The study was conducted as a randomized controlled trial with participants enrolled in sandwich programs at the University of Nigeria. Participants were divided into an intervention group that received weekly REBT sessions via WhatsApp and Zoom, and a control group that received motivational quotes and discussions on burnout. The REBT sessions focused on identifying and disputing irrational beliefs related to burnout, building resilience, and developing problem-solving skills. Data were collected at three points: pretest, posttest, and follow-up after three months. The researchers used the Oldenburg Burnout Inventory for Students (OLBI-S) to measure burnout levels.

The findings revealed that participants in the REBT intervention group showed significant reductions in burnout scores compared to the control group, both immediately after the intervention and at follow-up. This suggests that REBT is effective in managing burnout among adult learners who are teachers. "Our study extends the generalizability of REBT-based interventions to a new population," says Iremeka. Future research should explore the interaction between occupational and academic burnout and consider including adult learners who are not teachers to enhance generalizability. Additionally, multiple follow-up periods could help detect potential relapses over time.

Effects of Rational Emotive Behavior Occupational Intervention on Perceptions of Work Value and Ethical Practices: Implications for Educational Policy Makers [119]

This is a machine-generated summary of:

Abiogu, Godwin C.; Ede, Moses Onyemaechi; Agah, John J.; Ebeh, Jideofor Jeremiah; Ejionueme, Lambert K.; Asogwa, Emeka Timothy; Ekwueme, Francis Okechukwu; Agu, Patricia; Nwafor, Bernadette; Omeke, Faith; Ogoke, Jordan: Effects of Rational Emotive Behavior Occupational Intervention on Perceptions of Work Value and Ethical Practices: Implications for Educational Policy Makers [119]

Published in: Journal of Rational-Emotive & Cognitive-Behavior Therapy (2021)

Link to original: https://doi.org/10.1007/s10942-021-00389-0

If you want to cite the papers, please refer to the original.

For technical reasons we could not place the page where the original quote is coming from.

Research Highlights

Work values and work attitudes are fundamental elements that shape the operational culture of an organization and its employees. In the educational sector, these values are crucial for fostering a productive and ethical environment. However, in Nigeria, there has been a significant decline in work values among teachers, leading to unethical practices such as absenteeism, examination malpractices, and other forms of misconduct. Now a new study by Godwin C. Abiogu and colleagues investigates the effectiveness of Rational Emotive Behavioral Occupational Intervention (REBOI) in altering negative perceptions of work value and ethical practices among primary school teachers in Imo State, Southeast Nigeria.

The study employed a group-randomized control design involving 120 primary school teachers who were divided into treatment and control groups. The treatment group participated in an eight-week REBOI program, which included sessions on building therapeutic relationships, understanding work values, ethical practices, and cognitive-behavioral techniques. The intervention aimed to use the philosophies and techniques of Rational Emotive Behavioral Therapy (REBT) to alter false values and unrealistic ethical practices. According to Abiogu, "The REBOI program was designed to help teachers dispute their irrational beliefs about work demands and replace them with rational alternatives." The effectiveness of the intervention was measured using various scales such as the Organizational Values Scale (OVS), Ethical Sensitivity Scale (ESS), and Value Congruence Scale (VCS).

The findings revealed that the REBOI program significantly improved organizational values, ethical sensitivity, and value congruence among the participants in the treatment group compared to the control group. These improvements were sustained even at follow-up assessments. Abiogu notes, "Our study demonstrates that cognitive-behavioral modalities like REBOI can effectively change negatively skewed behavioral responses and enhance occupational well-being." The study suggests that integrating REBOI principles into teacher education curricula could improve work value systems and adherence to ethical practices among Nigerian teachers. Future research could explore the application of REBOI in other organizational settings to further validate its effectiveness.

Testing the Efficacy of Family Health-Model of REBT on Family Values and Quality of Family Life Among Parents of Children with Visual Impairment [120]

This is a machine-generated summary of:

Ede, Moses Onyemaechi; Okeke, Chinedu Ifedi; Chinweuba, Ngozi H.; Onah, Sebastian Okechukwu; Nwakpadolu, Glory M.: Testing the Efficacy of Family Health-Model of REBT on Family Values and Quality of Family Life Among Parents of Children with Visual Impairment [120]

Published in: Journal of Rational-Emotive & Cognitive-Behavior Therapy (2021)

Link to original: https://doi.org/10.1007/s10942-021-00409-z

If you want to cite the papers, please refer to the original.

For technical reasons we could not place the page where the original quote is coming from.

Research Highlights

Visual impairment in children significantly impacts their development and well-being, as well as the quality of life and family value of their parents. Previous studies have highlighted the emotional, psychological, and economic challenges faced by families of children with disabilities, often leading to poor quality of life and negative self-esteem among parents. Now a new study by Moses Onyemaechi Ede and colleagues investigates the efficacy of Rational Emotive Family Health Therapy (REFHT) in improving family values and quality of life among parents of children with visual impairment in Enugu State, Nigeria.

The study employed a randomized controlled design involving 120 Parents of children with visual impairment. Participants were randomly assigned to either the REFHT intervention group or a waitlisted control group. The intervention consisted of 12 weekly sessions focusing on altering irrational beliefs and improving coping strategies through techniques such as meditation, behavioral exercises, and motivational interviewing. The Family Value Scale (FVS) and Family Quality of

Life Scale (FQoL) were used to measure outcomes at pre-treatment, post-treatment, and follow-up stages. According to Ede, "The REFHT manual is designed to address psychological and social problems by using REBT approaches to alter irrational beliefs associated with low quality of family life."

The results demonstrated significant improvements in both family values and quality of life for participants in the REFHT group compared to the control group. These improvements were maintained at follow-up, indicating the long-term efficacy of the intervention. Ede notes that "the considerable long-term improvement observed among parents was attributed to the REFHT intervention." This study underscores the potential of cognitive-behavioral therapies like REFHT in addressing psychosocial challenges faced by families of children with disabilities. Future research could expand this approach to other regions and explore its impact on broader societal implications such as social withdrawal and mental health issues among family members.

Using REBT in the Treatment of Restless Leg Syndrome: A Case-Study [121]

This is a machine-generated summary of:

Newman, Chayim: Using REBT in the Treatment of Restless Leg Syndrome: A Case-Study [121]

Published in: Journal of Rational-Emotive & Cognitive-Behavior Therapy (2013)

Link to original: https://doi.org/10.1007/s10942-013-0174-z

If you want to cite the papers, please refer to the original.

For technical reasons we could not place the page where the original quote is coming from.

Research Highlights

Cognitive-behavioral therapies (CBT) have demonstrated efficacy in treating both primary psychological disorders and psychosomatic aspects of physiological disorders. However, the literature on the application of CBT in treating clients with restless leg syndrome (RLS) is limited, and there are currently no published studies on the treatment of RLS from a Rational Emotive Behavior Therapy (REBT) approach. Now, a new study by Chayim Newman and colleagues illustrates the use of REBT with positive outcomes in a client presenting with RLS.

In this case study, a 62-year-old married female of Indian descent sought treatment for chronic pain consistent with RLS, which had led to severely disturbed sleep and impaired daily functioning. The client had previously tried pharmacological treatments without success and was not on any medications at the time of the intervention. The therapeutic approach involved six sessions over an eight-week period, utilizing REBT to target irrational beliefs (IBs) about her RLS symptoms and incorporating behavioral interventions such as sleep hygiene and daily exercise. Quantitative measures were used to track progress, including the Outcome Questionnaire-45 (OQ-45) and a scale measuring rational and irrational beliefs.

The results were promising: over the course of treatment, the client reported a significant reduction in RLS symptoms, improved sleep quality, and enhanced daily functioning. By disputing IBs such as "I can't stand it when I don't have a full night of sleep" and replacing them with more rational beliefs like "I can handle it," the client experienced less distress and was able to implement behavioral changes effectively. At a follow-up three months post-treatment, she maintained these gains. This case study suggests that REBT may be a viable nonpharmacologic treatment for RLS, warranting further research through randomized controlled trials to establish broader empirical support.

Warrior Resilience and Thriving (WRT): Rational Emotive Behavior Therapy (REBT) as a Resiliency and Thriving Foundation to Prepare Warriors and Their Families for Combat Deployment and Posttraumatic Growth in Operation Iraqi Freedom, 2005–2009 [122]

This is a machine-generated summary of:

Jarrett, Thomas A.: Warrior Resilience and Thriving (WRT): Rational Emotive Behavior Therapy (REBT) as a Resiliency and Thriving Foundation to Prepare Warriors and Their Families for Combat Deployment and Posttraumatic Growth in Operation Iraqi Freedom, 2005–2009 [122]

Published in: Journal of Rational-Emotive & Cognitive-Behavior Therapy (2013)

Link to original: https://doi.org/10.1007/s10942-013-0163-2

If you want to cite the papers, please refer to the original.

For technical reasons we could not place the page where the original quote is coming from.

Research Highlights
The psychological resilience of military personnel is crucial for maintaining operational effectiveness and overall well-being. Despite the availability of mental health services, many soldiers avoid seeking help due to stigma and fear of being perceived as weak. Now a new study by Thomas A. Jarrett, an Albert Ellis Fellow and former Special Forces Non-commissioned Officer, addresses this issue by

implementing Rational Emotive Behavior Therapy (REBT) in a combat environment to enhance resilience among soldiers.

Jarrett's study involved the development and deployment of the Warrior Resilience Training (WRT) program during Operation Iraqi Freedom. The program was designed to teach soldiers REBT principles, which emphasize rational thinking and emotional regulation, to help them manage combat stress and other challenges. Jarrett's team trained over 5000 soldiers using a standardized 90-minute class that incorporated real-world examples from combat scenarios. Feedback from participants indicated high acceptance and perceived utility of the training, with many soldiers reporting improved emotional management and resilience.

The main advance of this study is the successful adaptation of REBT for use in a military context, demonstrating its potential to reduce combat-related stress and improve mental health outcomes. Jarrett notes that "REBT's straightforward, research-based approach appeals to professional soldiers who value efficiency and practical solutions." Future directions include expanding the WRT program to include family members and further integrating it into formal Army resiliency initiatives like the Comprehensive Soldier Fitness Master Resilience Trainer Program. This study underscores the importance of tailored psychological interventions in enhancing the resilience of military personnel and their families.

Rational Emotive Behavior Therapy Successes and Failures: Eight Personal Perspectives [123]

This is a machine-generated summary of:

Weinrach, Stephen G.; Ellis, Albert; MacLaren, Catharine; DiGiuseppe, Raymond; Vernon, Ann; Wolfe, Janet; Malkinson, Ruth; Backx, Wouter: Rational emotive behavior therapy successes and failures: Eight personal perspectives [123]

Published in: Journal of Rational-Emotive & Cognitive-Behavior Therapy (2006)

Link to original: https://doi.org/10.1007/s10942-006-0047-9

If you want to cite the papers, please refer to the original.

For technical reasons we could not place the page where the original quote is coming from.

Research Highlights

Rational Emotive Behavior Therapy (REBT) is a well-regarded theory of mental health and philosophy of life, emphasizing the importance of rational thinking in managing emotions and behaviors. Despite its efficacy, even experts in REBT are not immune to emotional and behavioral overreactions. Now, a new study by Stephen G. Weinrach and colleagues from the Albert Ellis Institute's International Training Standards Committee explores how REBT experts apply the therapy to themselves, revealing both successes and failures.

The study involved eight committee members from various countries who were asked to write two essays: one detailing a successful application of REBT in their lives and another describing a failure. The responses were compiled, edited for consistency, and analyzed for common themes. The narratives revealed that even seasoned REBT practitioners struggle with irrational beliefs and emotional challenges. For instance, while some experts successfully managed anxiety or practiced unconditional other-acceptance using REBT techniques, others faced difficulties with low frustration tolerance or self-acceptance. The study highlighted that rational self-talk was more prevalent in successful cases, whereas irrational beliefs like "shoulds" and "musts" dominated the failures.

The findings underscore that the effective use of REBT requires continuous effort and is not universally applicable to every situation. As Weinrach notes, "The successful use of REBT requires considerable and continuous hard work." This research suggests that while REBT can be a powerful tool for managing emotions and behaviors, it is not infallible, even for its most knowledgeable practitioners. Future research could explore additional strategies to enhance the efficacy of REBT or investigate how combining it with other therapeutic approaches might benefit individuals facing complex emotional challenges.

Trait Anger and Axis I Disorders: Implications for REBT [124]

This is a machine-generated summary of:

McDermut, Wilson; Fuller, J. Ryan; DiGiuseppe, Raymond; Chelminski, Iwona; Zimmerman, Mark: Trait Anger and Axis I Disorders: Implications for REBT [124]

Published in: Journal of Rational-Emotive & Cognitive-Behavior Therapy (2009)

Link to original: https://doi.org/10.1007/s10942-009-0092-2

If you want to cite the papers, please refer to the original.

For technical reasons we could not place the page where the original quote is coming from.

Research Highlights

Although anger is a universal and normal aspect of human experience, research over the last two to three decades has shown that anger can also be problematic and dysfunctional. Anger can lead to aggressive behaviors, resulting in negative outcomes such as arguments or property damage. Now, a new study by Wilson McDermut and colleagues aims to evaluate the validity of an anger diagnosis in psychiatric outpatients by examining co-occurrence rates with other disorders.

The study involved 1000 psychiatric outpatients who participated in the Rhode Island Methods to Improve Diagnosis and Services project. High levels of trait anger served as a proxy for an anger diagnosis. Participants were assessed using the Structured Clinical Interview for DSM-IV Disorders (SCID) and the Structured Interview for DSM-IV Personality (SIDP). The researchers found that high trait anger was associated with a diverse range of Axis I disorders but was not subsumed by any single diagnosis. "Interestingly, 30% of the high trait anger participants did not also have a diagnosis of one of the angry/aggressive Axis I disorders or Borderline Personality Disorder (BPD) or Antisocial Personality Disorder (ASPD)," McDermut notes. The study also revealed that high trait anger was linked to more psychiatric morbidity and psychosocial impairment.

The findings suggest that high trait anger is a significant predictor of psychiatric morbidity and psychosocial functioning, independent of other Axis I diagnoses. "Our data point to the importance of recognizing and addressing anger problems in clinical populations," McDermut emphasizes. Future research should focus on developing reliable diagnostic methods for anger disorders and exploring their treatment implications. The study underscores the need for clinicians to prioritize the assessment of anger alongside depression and anxiety, potentially leading to more effective interventions for individuals with primary anger disorders.

Effect of Rational Emotive Behavior Therapy Program on Depressive Symptoms Among University Students with Blindness in Nigeria [125]

This is a machine-generated summary of:

Onuigbo, Liziana N.; Eseadi, Chiedu; Ebifa, Samuel; Ugwu, Uchenna Cosmas; Onyishi, Charity N.; Oyeoku, Eke Kalu: Effect of Rational Emotive Behavior Therapy Program on Depressive Symptoms Among University Students with Blindness in Nigeria [125]

Published in: Journal of Rational-Emotive & Cognitive-Behavior Therapy (2018)

Link to original: https://doi.org/10.1007/s10942-018-0297-3

If you want to cite the papers, please refer to the original.

For technical reasons we could not place the page where the original quote is coming from.

Research Highlights

Depression is a major public health challenge among university students, with a particularly high prevalence in Nigeria. Blind students face unique challenges that may increase their risk of depression, including mobility issues, social isolation, and academic pressures. Now, a new study by Liziana N. Onuigbo and colleagues investigates the efficacy of group-based Rational Emotive Behavior Therapy (REBT) in reducing depressive symptoms among blind university students in Nigeria.

The study employed a group randomized controlled trial design involving pretest, posttest, and follow-up evaluations. A total of 60 blind students were randomly assigned to either an REBT treatment group or a no-intervention control group. The REBT program consisted of weekly sessions over eight weeks, followed by bi-weekly follow-up meetings for three months. The Beck Depression Inventory-II (BDI-II) was used to measure depressive symptoms at baseline, post-treatment, and follow-up. According to Onuigbo, "The REBT program aimed to help participants develop rational thinking skills and cope with depressive thoughts through cognitive, emotive, and behavioral techniques."

The results showed a significant reduction in depressive symptoms among participants in the REBT treatment group compared to the control group. This reduction was maintained during the follow-up period, indicating the sustainability of the intervention's effects. Onuigbo notes that "the effectiveness of the REBT intervention suggests that it could be a viable treatment option for managing depression among blind students." Future research should explore the long-term impact of REBT and consider including measures of irrational beliefs alongside depression scales to provide a more comprehensive assessment of its efficacy.

Bibliography

1. Ellis, A. (1994). *Reason and emotion in psychotherapy*. Birch Lane.
2. Brown, D., & Crace, R. K. (1996). *Life values inventory*. Life Values Resources.
3. Vernon, A., & Bernard, M. E. (2019). Rational emotive behavior education in schools. In M. E. Bernard & W. Dryden (Eds.), *Advances in REBT*. Springer. https://doi.org/10.1007/978-3-319-93118-0_13
4. APA Presidential Task Force on Evidence-Based Practice. (2006). Evidence-based practice in psychology. *American Psychologist, 61*, 271–285.
5. Meaden, A., Keen, N., Aston, R., Barton, K., & Bucci, S. (2013). *Cognitive therapy for command hallucinations: An advanced practical companion*. Routledge.
6. Gaviţa, O. A., David, D., Bujoreanu, S., Tiba, A., & Ionuţiu, D. R. (2012). The efficacy of a short cognitive–behavioral parent program in the treatment of externalizing behavior disorders in Romanian foster care children: Building parental emotion-regulation through unconditional self-and child-acceptance strategies. *Children and Youth Services Review, 34*(7), 1290–1297.

7. Stefan, S., Cristea, I. A., Szentagotai Tatar, A., & David, D. (2019). Cognitive-behavioral therapy (CBT) for generalized anxiety disorder: Contrasting various CBT approaches in a randomized clinical trial. *Journal of Clinical Psychology*, *75*(7), 1188–1202.
8. Szentagotai, A., & Freeman, A. (2007). An analysis of the relationship between irrational beliefs and automatic thoughts in predicting distress. *Journal of Cognitive & Behavioral Psychotherapies*, *7*(1).
9. Ellis, A. (1994). *Reason and emotion in psychotherapy (Re)*. Birch Lane.
10. Jacobson, N. S., & Truax, P. (1991). Clinical significance: A statistical approach to defining meaningful change in psychotherapy research. *Journal of Consulting and Clinical Psychology*, *59*(1), 12.
11. Jacobson, N. S., Roberts, L. J., Berns, S. B., & McGlinchey, J. B. (1999). Methods for defining and determining the clinical significance of treatment effects: Description, application, and alternatives. *Journal of Consulting and Clinical Psychology*, *67*(3), 300.
12. Bernard, M. E. (1998). Validation of the General Attitude and Belief Scale. *Journal of Rational-Emotive & Cognitive-Behavior Therapy*, *16*, 183–196.
13. DiGiuseppe, R. D., Dryden, W., & Backx, W. (2014). *A practitioners' guide to rational emotive behavior therapy*, (3rd ed). Oxford University Press.
14. Carey, M. P., & Schroder, K. E. E. (2002). Development and psychometric evaluation of the brief HIV knowledge questionnaire (HIV-KQ-18). *AIDS Education and Prevention*, *14*, 174–184.
15. Napper, E., Fisher, D. G., & Reynolds, G. L. (2012). Development of the perceived risk of HIV scale. *AIDS and Behaviour*, *16*(40), 1075–1083.
16. Ezegbe, B. N., Eseadi, C., Ede, M. O., Igbo, J. N., Aneke, A., Mezieobi, D., et al. (2018). Efficacy of rational emotive digital storytelling intervention on knowledge and risk perception of HIV/AIDS among schoolchildren in Nigeria. *Medicine*, *97*(47), e12910.
17. Lee, J. H., Schell, M. J., & Roetzheim, R. (2009). Analysis of group randomized trials with multiple binary endpoints and small number of groups. *PLoS ONE*, *4*(10), e7265.
18. Kelley, B. C. (2007). *Journey through stress*. Performance Enhancement Group.
19. Pretzer, L., Beck, A., & Newman, C. (2002). Stress and stress management: A cognitive view. In R. Leahy & E. Dowd (Eds.), *Clinical advances in cognitive psychotherapy: Theory and application* (pp. 163–179). Springer.
20. Klarreich, S. H., DiGiuseppe, R., & DiMattia, D. J. (1987). Cost effectiveness of an employee assistance program with rational-emotive therapy. *Professional Psychology: Research and Practice*, *18*(2), 140–144.
21. Sava, F. A., Yates, B. T., Lupu, V., Szentagotai, A., & David, D. (2009). Cost-effectiveness and cost-utility of cognitive therapy, rational emotive behavioral therapy, and fluoxetine (Prozac) in treating depression: A randomized clinical trial. *Journal of Clinical Psychology*, *65*(1), 36–52.
22. Brown, J. D. (2007). Sample size and power. Shiken: JALT testing & evaluation SIG newsletter, 11(1), 31–35. Retrieved from http://jalt.org/test/bro_25.html. Accessed 08 June 2015.
23. Ellis, A. (1994). *Reason and emotion in psychotherapy* (Rev. ed.). Birch Lane.
24. Blayney, J. A., Read, J. P., & Colder, C. (2016). Role of alcohol in college sexual victimization and post assault adaptation. *Psychological Trauma: Theory, Research, Practice, and Policy*, *8*(4), 421–430. https://doi.org/10.1037/tra0000100
25. Ellis, A. (2001). *Overcoming destructive beliefs, feelings, and behaviors: New directions for rational emotivebehavior therapy*. Prometheus Books.
26. Maclaren, C., Doyle, K. A., & Digiuseppe, R. (2016). *Rational emotive behavior therapy (REBT) Theoryand Practice*. Sage Publications.
27. Wood, A. G., Turner, M. J., Barker, J. B., & Higgins, S. J. (2017). Investigating the effects of irrational and rational self-statements on motor-skill and hazard-perception performance. *Sport, Exercise, and Performance Psychology*, *6*(4), 384–400. https://doi.org/10.1037/spy0000095

28. Marić, Z. (2002). Kognitivni činioci emocije i emocionalnog poremećaja iz ugla REBT (magistarska teza).Beograd: Odeljenje za psihologiju, Filozofski fakultet. [Cognitive factors of emotion and emotional disorder from the REBT point of view. Master's thesis. Belgrade: Department of Psychology, Faculty of Philosophy.]
29. Marić, Z. (2003). Uloga disfunkcionalnih stavova u depresivnom raspoloženju i provera medijacionog efekta "'vrelih"' evaluativnih kognicija [The role of dysfunctional attitudes in depressive mood and the mediation effect of "'hot"' evaluative cognitions]. *Psihologija*, *36*(1), 101–115. https://doi.org/10.2298/PSI0301101M
30. DiGiuseppe, R., Leaf, R., Exner, T., & Robin, M. (1988). The development of a measure of irrational/rational thinking. Paper presented at the World congress of behavior therapy, Edinburgh, Scotland.
31. Vukosavljevic-Gvozden, T., Filipovic, S., & Opacic, G. (2015). The mediating role of symptoms of psychopathology between irrational beliefs and internet gaming addiction. *Journal of Rational-Emotive & Cognitive-Behavior Therapy*, *33*(4), 387–405. https://doi.org/10.1007/s10942-015-0218-7
32. Gorgu, N. S., & Sutcu, S. T. (2016). Effectiveness of cognitive behavioral group therapy for treatment of dysfunctional anger: A systematic review. *Current Approaches in Psychiatry*, *8*(1), 129–143.
33. Bakare, J., Omeje, H. O., Yisa, M. A., Orji, C. T., Onyechi, K. C., Eseadi, C., Nwajiuba, C. A., & Anyaegbunam, E. N. (2019). Investigation of burnout syndrome among electrical and building technology undergraduate students in Nigeria. *Medicine*, *98*(42), e17581.
34. Ede, M. O., Anyanwu, J. I., Onuigbo, L. N., Ifelunni, C. O., Alabi-Oparaocha, F. C., Okenyi, E. C., et al. (2020). Rational emotive family health therapy for reducing parenting stress in families of children with autism spectrum disorders: A group randomized control study. *Journal of Rational-Emotive & Cognitive-Behavior Therapy*. https://doi.org/10.1007/s10942-020-00342-7
35. Nwabuko, L. O., Okechukwu, A. E., Eneh, E. C., Eze, G. C., & Eseabasi, F. O. (2020). Effect of a cognitive behavioural intervention on depression reduction among community-dwelling adult learners in Nigeria: Implications for adult education administration. *Journal of International Medical Research*, *48*(1), 0300060519885558.
36. Times Higher Education. (2020). University of Nigeria Nsukka. Retrieved from http://www.timeshighereducation.com/world-university-rankings/university-nigeria-nsukka
37. Igbokwe, U. L., Nwokenna, E. N., Eseadi, C., Ogbonna, C. S., Nnadi, E. M., Ololo, K. O., Enyoghasim, O. M., Otu, O. A., Uma, K. E., Onuora, T. N., Onwube, O., & Ogbuagu, A. R. (2019). Intervention for burnout among English education undergraduates: Implications for curriculum innovation. *Medicine*, *98*(26), e16219.
38. Igbokwe, U. L., Onyechi, K. C., Ogbonna, C. S., Eseadi, C., Onwuegbuchulam, A. C., Nwajiuba, C. A., Ugodulunwa, C. C., Eze, A., Omaeze, K., Patrick, C. P., Ekechukwu, L. E., Egbe, C. I., Nnachi, R. A., & Anyaegbunam, E. N. (2019). Rational emotive intervention for stress management among english education undergraduates: Implications for school curriculum innovation. *Medicine*, *98*(40), e17452.
39. Tabachnick, B. G., & Fidell, L. S. (2012). *Using multivariate statistics* (6th ed). Pearson. https://www.statisticssolutions.com/directory-of-statistical-analyses-manova-analysis/
40. Ntamu, B. A. (2017). Effect of rational emotive behavioural therapy on curbing examination malpractice behaviour among public secondary school students in Calabar municipality. *International Journal of Scientific Research in Education*, *10*(4), 440–450.
41. Heimberg, R. G. (2002). Cognitive-behavioral therapy for social anxiety disorder: Current status and future directions. *Biological Psychiatry*, *51*(1), 101–108.
42. Grumet, R., & Fitzpatrick, M. (2016). A case for integrating values clarification work into cognitive behavioral therapy for social anxiety disorder. *Journal of Psychotherapy Integration*, *26*(1), 11–21.

43. Lupón, M., Armayones, M., & Cardona, G. (2018). Quality of life among parents of children with visual impairment: A literature Review. *Research In Developmental Disabilities*. https://doi.org/10.1016/j.ridd.2018.08.013
44. Weiss, J. A., Viecili, M. A., & Bohr, Y. (2015). Parenting stress as a correlate of cognitive behavior therapy responsiveness in children with autism spectrum disorders and anxiety. *Focus on Autism and Other Developmental Disabilities*, *30*(3), 154–164.
45. Murphy, N. A., Christian, B., Caplin, D. A., & Young, P. C. (2007). The health of caregivers for children with disabilities: Caregiver perspectives. *Child Care, Health and Development*, *33*, 180–187.
46. Sanders, M. R. (2012). Development, evaluation, and multinational dissemination of the triple p-positive parenting program. *Annual Review of Clinical Psychology*, *8*, 345–379.
47. Ede, M. O., Omeje, C. J., Ncheke, D. C., Agah, J. J., Chinweuba, N. H., & Amoke, C. V. (2020). Assessment of the effectiveness of group cognitive behavioural therapy in reducing pathological gambling. *Journal of Gambling Studies*. https://doi.org/10.1007/s10899-020-09981-y
48. Pigeon, W. R., & Yurcheshen, M. (2009). Behavioral sleep medicine interventions for restless legs syndrome and periodic limb movement disorder. *Sleep Medicine Clinics*, *4*, 549–558.
49. Edinger, J. D., Fins, A. I., Sullivan, R. J., et al. (1996). Comparison of cognitive-behavioral therapy and clonazepam for treating periodic limb movement disorder. *Sleep*, *19*(5), 442–444.
50. Hornyak, M., Grossmann, C., Kohnen, R., et al. (2008). Cognitive behavioural group therapy to improve patients' strategies for coping with restless legs syndrome: A proof-of-concept trial. *Journal of Neurology, Neurosurgery & Psychiatry*, *79*, 823–825.
51. Lindner, H., Kirkby, R., Wertheim, E., & Birch, P. (1999). A brief assessment of irrational thinking: The shortened General Attitude and Belief Scale. *Cognitive Therapy and Research*, *23*(6), 651–663. https://doi.org/10.1023/A:1018741009293
52. Fishman, D. (2005). Editor's introduction to PCSP—from single case to database: A new method for enhancing psychotherapy practice. Pragmatic Case Studies in Psychotherapy, 1(1). Retrieved September 22, 2013, from http://reaper64.scc-net.rutgers.edu/journals/index.php/pcsp/article/view/855/2168.
53. Ellis, A. (1962). *Reason and emotion in psychotherapy*. Citadel.
54. Office of The Surgeon General. (2009, May). *Mental Health Advisory Team (MHAT) VI Operation Iraqi Freedom 07–09*. United States Army Medical Command.
55. Hoge, C., Auchetrlonie, J., & Milliken, C. (2009). Mental health problems, use of mental health services and attrition from military service after returning from deployment to Iraq and Afghanistan. *Journal of the American Medical Association*, *295*(9), 1023–1035.
56. McFarlane, A. C. (2009). Military deployment: The impact on children and family adjustment and the need for care. *Current Opinion in Psychiatry*, 22,369–373.
57. David, D., Szentagotai, A., Eva, K., & Macavei, B. (2005). A synopsis of rational-emotive behavior therapy (REBT); fundamental and applied research. *Journal of Rational-Emotive & Cognitive-Behavior Therapy*, *23*(3), 175–221.
58. Ellis, A. (1962, /1993). *Reason and emotion in psychotherapy*. Lyle Stewart/Birch Lane Press.
59. Ellis, A. (1996a). *Better, deeper, and more enduring brief therapy: The rational emotive behavior therapy approach*. Brunner/Mazel.
60. Ellis, A. (1996b). How I learned to help clients feel better and get better. *Psychotherapy*, *33*(1), 149–151.
61. Resick, P. (1992). Cognitive therapy for posttraumatic stress disorder. *Journal of Cognitive Psychotherapy*, *15*(4), 321–329.
62. Hadot, P., & Chase, P. (2001). *The inner citadel: The meditations of marcus aurelius*. Harvard University Press.
63. Long, A. (2002). *Epictetus: A stoic and socratic guide to life*. Oxford University Press.

64. Inwood, B. (Ed.). (2003). *The Cambridge companion to the Stoics*. University Press.
65. Khoshaba, S. C., Maddi, S. R., & Kahn, S. (1982). Hardiness and health: A prospective study. *Journal of Personal and Social Psychology, 42*(1), 168–177.
66. Bartone, P. (1999, Spring). Hardiness predicts against war-related stress in reserve units. *Consulting Psychology Journal: Practice and Research.*
67. Khoshaba, S. C., & Maddi, S. R. (2005). *Resilience at work: How to succeed no matter what life throws at you.* AMACOM.
68. Frankl, V. E. (1963). *Man's search for meaning*. Beacon Press.
69. Siebert, A. (1996). *The survivor personality*. Penguin Putnam.
70. Siebert, A. (2005). *The resiliency advantage: Master change, thrive under pressure, and bounce back from setbacks*. Berrett-Koehler.
71. Basu, M. (2006). *Georgia's guard: The 48th in Iraq: Stoicism gives troops "armor for the soul"*. Atlanta Journal Constitution.
72. Mott, M. (2006, June 25). Learning Stoic 'ABCs:' Warrior resilience training helps soldiers maintain mental, emotional health in Iraq. *The Ivy Leaf, 1*, 11.
73. Jarrett, T. (2008). Warrior resilience training in operation Iraqi freedom: Combining rational emotive behavior therapy, resiliency, and positive psychology. *The United States Army Medical Department Journal*, 32–38.
74. Gomez, J. (2009). *Military puts focus on epidemic of suicides*. USA Today. April.
75. Sherman, N. (2009). *The untold war: Inside the hearts, minds and souls of our soldiers*. W.W. Norton.
76. Frankl, V. E. (1986). *The doctor and the soul: From psychotherapy to logotherapy*. Vintage.
77. Boone, R., Camarillo, C., Landry, L., & DeLucia, J. (2008). Army provider resiliency training: Healing the wounds "on the inside. *The United States Army Medical Department Journal*, 32–38.
78. Figley, C. R. (Ed.). (1995). *Compassion fatigue: Secondary traumatic stress disorders from treating the traumatized*. Brunner/Mazel.
79. Stamm, B. (2002). Measuring compassion satisfaction as well as fatigue: Developmental history of the compassion satisfaction and fatigue test. In C. R. Figley (Ed.), *Treating compassion fatigue* (pp. 107–119). Brunner-Routledge.
80. Deffenbacher, J., Oetting, E., Lynch, R., & Morris, C. (1996). The expression of emotion and its consequences. *Behaviour Research and Therapy, 34*, 575–590.
81. Anderson, C. A., & Bushman, B. J. (2002). Human aggression. *Annual Review of Psychology, 53*, 27–51.
82. Baumeister, R. F., Smart, L., & Boden, J. (1996). Relation of threatened egotism to violence and aggression: The dark side of high self-esteem. *Psychological Review, 103*, 5–33.
83. Averill, J. R. (1983). Studies on anger and aggression: Implications for theories of emotion. *American Psychologist, 38*, 1145–1160.
84. Kassinove, H., Sukhodolsky, D., Tsytsarev, S., & Solovyova, S. (1997). Self-reported anger episodes in Russia and America. *Journal of Social Behavior and Personality, 12*, 301–324.
85. Tafrate, R. C., Kassinove, H., & Dundin, L. (2002). Anger episodes in high and low trait anger community adults. *Journal of Clinical Psychology, 58*, 1573–1590.
86. Kassinove, H., Roth, D., Owens, S. G., & Fuller, J. R. (2002). Effects of trait anger and anger expression style on competitive attack responses in a wartime prisoner's dilemma game. *Aggressive Behavior, 28*, 117–125.
87. Deffenbacher, J. (2000, August). Characteristics of individuals high in driving anger: Prevention and intervention. Paper presented at the 108th annual convention of the American Psychological Association, Washington, DC.
88. Kassinove, H., & Tafrate, R. C. (2006). *Anger management video program: An instructional guide for practitioners*. Impact Publishers.

89. DiGiuseppe, R., & Tafrate, R. C. (2004). *Anger disorders scale: Manual*. Multi Health Systems.
90. Pfohl, B., Blum, N., & Zimmerman, M. (1997). *Structured interview for DSM-IV personality*. American Psychiatric Press.
91. Eckhardt, C. I., & Deffenbacher, J. L. (1995). Diagnosis of anger disorders. In H. Kassinove (Ed.), *Anger disorders: Definition, diagnosis and treatment* (pp. 27–47). Taylor & Francis.
92. Sava, F., Yates, B., Lupu, V., Szentagotai, A., & David, D. (2009). Cost-effectiveness and cost-utility of cognitive therapy, rational–emotive–behavior therapy, and fluoxetine (prozac) in treating depression: A randomized clinical trial. *Journal of Clinical Psychology, 65*(1), 36–52.
93. Brody, B. L., Gamst, A. C., Williams, R. A., Smith, A. R., Lau, P. W., Dolnak, D., et al. (2001). Depression, visual acuity, comorbidity, and disability associated with age-related macular degeneration. *Ophthalmology, 108*(10), 1893–1900.
94. Evans, J. R., Fletcher, A. E., & Wormald, R. P. (2007). Depression and anxiety in visually impaired older people. *Ophthalmology, 114*(2), 283–288.
95. Rovner, B. W., Casten, R. J., & Tasman, W. S. (2002). Effect of depression on vision function in age-related macular degeneration. *Archives of Ophthalmology, 120*(8), 1041–1044.
96. Stevelink, S. A., & Fear, N. T. (2016). Psychosocial impact of visual impairment and coping strategies in female ex-service personnel. *Journal of the Royal Army Medical Corps*. https://doi.org/10.1136/jramc-2015-000518
97. Reinhardt, J. P. (2001). Effects of positive and negative support received and provided on adaptation to chronic visual impairment. *Applied Developmental Science, 5*(2), 76–85.
98. Bragg, M. W. (2005). Vision loss, depression and rehabilitation. *International Congress Series, 1282*, 40–41. https://doi.org/10.1016/j.ics.2005.06.028
99. Horowitz, A., Reinhardt, J. P., & Kennedy, G. J. (2005b). Major and subthreshold depression among older adults seeking vision rehabilitation services. *The American Journal of Geriatric Psychiatry, 13*(3), 180–187.
100. Hayman, K. J., Kerse, N. M., La Grow, S. J., Wouldes, T., Robertson, M. C., & Campbell, A. J. (2007). Depression in older people: Visual impairment and subjective ratings of health. *Optometry and Vision Science, 84*(11), 1024–1030.
101. Renaud, J., Levasseur, M., Gresset, J., Overbury, O., Wanet-Defalque, M. C., Dubois, M. F., et al. (2010). Health-related and subjective quality of life of older adults with visual impairment. *Disability and Rehabilitation, 32*(11), 899–907.
102. DiGiuseppe, R., Doyle, K. A., & Rose, R. D. (2002). Rational emotive behaviour therapy for depression: Achieving unconditional self-acceptance. In M. A. Reinecke & M. R. Davison (Eds.), *Comparative treatments of depression* (pp. 220–228). Springer.
103. David, D., Kangas, M., Schnur, J. B., & Montgomery, G. H. (2004). *REBT depression manual: Managing depression using rational emotive behavior therapy*. Babes-Bolyai University.
104. Jalali, M. D. M., Moussavi, M. S., Yazdi, S. A. A., & Fadardi, J. S. (2014). Effectiveness of rational emotive behavior therapy on psychological well-being of people with late blindness. *Journal of Rational-Emotive & Cognitive-Behavior Therapy, 32*(4), 233–247.
105. Ogbuanya, T. C., Eseadi, C., Orji, C. T., Omeje, J. C., Anyanwu, J. I., Ugwoke, S. C., & Edeh, N. C. (2019). Effect of rational-emotive behavior therapy program on the symptoms of burnout syndrome among undergraduate electronics work students in Nigeria. *Psychological Reports, 122*(1), 4–22.
106. Ogbuanya, T. C., Eseadi, C., Orji, C. T., Anyanwu, J. I., Ede, M. O., & Bakare, J. (2017). Effect of rational-emotive behavior therapy on negative career thoughts of students in technical colleges in Nigeria. *Psychological Reports*. https://doi.org/10.1177/0033294117724449

107. Ogbuanya, T. C., Eseadi, C., Orji, C. T., Anyanwu, J. I., Joachim, O. C., & Otu, M. S. (2017b). The effect of rational emotive behavior therapy on irrational career beliefs of students of electrical electronics and other engineering trades in technical colleges in Nigeria. *Journal of Rational-Emotive & Cognitive-Behavior Therapy*. https://doi.org/10.1007/s10942-017-0282-2
108. Eseadi, C., Obidoa, M. A., Ogbuabor, S. E., & Ikechuwu-Ilomuanya, A. B. (2017). Effects of group-focused cognitive-behavioral coaching program on depressive symptoms in a sample of inmates in a Nigerian prison. *International Journal of Offender Therapy and Comparative Criminology*. https://doi.org/10.1177/0306624X16687046
109. Eseadi, C., Onwuka, G. T., Otu, M. S., Umoke, P. I., Onyechi, K. C. N., Okere, A. U., et al. (2017). Effects of rational emotive cognitive behavioural coaching on depression among type 2 diabetic inpatients. *Journal of Rational-Emotive & Cognitive-Behavior Therapy, 35*(4), 363–382.
110. Ugwoke, S. C., Eseadi, C., Igbokwe, C. C., Chiaha, G. T., Nwaubani, O. O., Orji, C. T., et al. (2017). Effects of a rational-emotive health education intervention on stress management and irrational beliefs among technical college teachers in southeast Nigeria. *Medicine, 96*(31), e7658. https://doi.org/10.1097/MD.0000000000007658
111. Abiogu, G. C., Ede, M. O., Mezieobi, D. I., Nwosu, N., Ogheneakoke, C. E., Ujah, P., Chukwuemeka, E. A., & Agbigwe, I. B. (2021). Reducing negative value system in students: The impacts of rational emotive behavioural education. *Journal of Rational-Emotive & Cognitive-Behavior Therapy*. https://doi.org/10.1007/s10942-021-00387-2
112. Artiran, M., & DiGiuseppe, R. (2021). Rational emotive behavior therapy compared to client-centered therapy for outpatients: A randomized clinical trial with a three months follow up. *Journal of Rational-Emotive & Cognitive-Behavior Therapy*. https://doi.org/10.1007/s10942-021-00408-0
113. Ezegbe, B. N., Eseadi, C., Ede, M. O., Igbo, J. N., Aneke, A., Nnamani, A., Ugwu, G. C., Ugwoezuonu, A. U., Elizabeth, E., Ede, K. R., Chinweuba, N. H., & Ede, A. O. (2019). Rational emotive digital storytelling therapy for improving HIV/AIDS knowledge and risk perception among schoolchildren: A group randomized trial. *Journal of Rational-Emotive & Cognitive-Behavior Therapy*. https://doi.org/10.1007/s10942-019-00316-4
114. Eseadi, C., Anyanwu, J. I., Ogbuabor, S. E., & Ikechukwu-Ilomuanya, A. B. (2015). Effects of cognitive restructuring intervention program of rational-emotive behavior therapy on adverse childhood stress in Nigeria. *Journal of Rational-Emotive & Cognitive-Behavior Therapy*. https://doi.org/10.1007/s10942-015-0229-4
115. Ede, M. O., Adene, F. M., Okeke, C. I., Mezieobi, D. I., Isiwu, E. N., & Abdullahi, Y. (2021). The effect of rational emotive behaviour therapy on post-traumatic depression in flood victims. *Journal of Rational-Emotive & Cognitive-Behavior Therapy*. https://doi.org/10.1007/s10942-021-00401-7
116. Stojković, I., Vukosavljević-Gvozden, T., David, I., & Purić, D. (2022). Internet addiction in adolescents: A rational emotive and cognitive behavior therapy perspective. *Journal of Rational-Emotive & Cognitive-Behavior Therapy*. https://doi.org/10.1007/s10942-022-00445-3
117. Kabadayi, F., & Yuksel, G. (2021). Rational-emotive behavior therapy for dysfunctional anger: A case study. *Journal of Rational-Emotive & Cognitive-Behavior Therapy*. https://doi.org/10.1007/s10942-020-00384-x
118. Iremeka, F. U., Eseadi, C., Ezenwaji, C., Ezenwaji, I. O., Okide, C. C., Ogbonna, C. S., & Onwuchekwe, S. I. (2021). Effect of school-based rational-emotive behaviour program on burnout among adult learners: Moderating influence of participants' demographic variables. *Journal of Rational-Emotive & Cognitive-Behavior Therapy*. https://doi.org/10.1007/s10942-021-00393-4
119. Abiogu, G. C., Ede, M. O., Agah, J. J., Ebeh, J. J., Ejionueme, L. K., Asogwa, E. T., Ekwueme, F. O., Agu, P., Nwafor, B., Omeke, F., & Ogoke, J. (2021). Effects of rational emotive behavior occupational intervention on perceptions of work value and ethical

practices: Implications for educational policy makers. *Journal of Rational-Emotive & Cognitive-Behavior Therapy*. https://doi.org/10.1007/s10942-021-00389-0
120. Ede, M. O., Okeke, C. I., Chinweuba, N. H., Onah, S. O., & Nwakpadolu, G. M. (2021). Testing the efficacy of family health-model of REBT on family values and quality of family life among parents of children with visual impairment. *Journal of Rational-Emotive & Cognitive-Behavior Therapy*. https://doi.org/10.1007/s10942-021-00409-z
121. Newman, C. (2013). Using REBT in the treatment of restless leg syndrome: A case-study. *Journal of Rational-Emotive & Cognitive-Behavior Therapy*. https://doi.org/10.1007/s10942-013-0174-z
122. Jarrett, T. A. (2013). Warrior resilience and thriving (WRT): Rational emotive behavior therapy (REBT) as a resiliency and thriving foundation to prepare warriors and their families for combat deployment and posttraumatic growth in operation Iraqi Freedom, 2005–2009. *Journal of Rational-Emotive & Cognitive-Behavior Therapy*. https://doi.org/10.1007/s10942-013-0163-2
123. Weinrach, S. G., Ellis, A., MacLaren, C., DiGiuseppe, R., Vernon, A., Wolfe, J., Malkinson, R., & Backx, W. (2006). Rational emotive behavior therapy successes and failures: Eight personal perspectives. *Journal of Rational-Emotive & Cognitive-Behavior Therapy*. https://doi.org/10.1007/s10942-006-0047-9
124. McDermut, W., Fuller, J. R., DiGiuseppe, R., Chelminski, I., & Zimmerman, M. (2009). Trait anger and Axis I disorders: Implications for REBT. *Journal of Rational-Emotive & Cognitive-Behavior Therapy*. https://doi.org/10.1007/s10942-009-0092-2
125. Onuigbo, L. N., Eseadi, C., Ebifa, S., Ugwu, U. C., Onyishi, C. N., & Oyeoku, E. K. (2018). Effect of rational emotive behavior therapy program on depressive symptoms among University students with blindness in Nigeria. *Journal of Rational-Emotive & Cognitive-Behavior Therapy*. https://doi.org/10.1007/s10942-018-0297-3

MIX
Papier aus verantwortungsvollen Quellen
Paper from responsible sources
FSC® C105338

If you have any concerns about our products,
you can contact us on
ProductSafety@springernature.com

In case Publisher is established outside the EU,
the EU authorized representative is:
Springer Nature Customer Service Center GmbH
Europaplatz 3, 69115 Heidelberg, Germany

Printed by Libri Plureos GmbH
in Hamburg, Germany